MURDER & MAYHEM
IN
HOUSTON

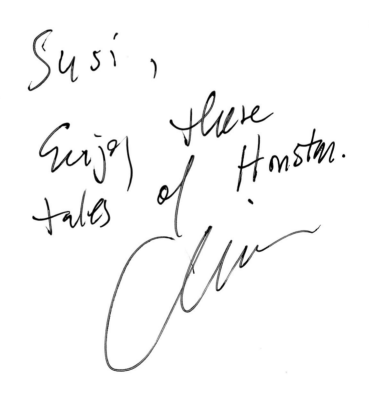

Susi,

Enjoy these
tales of Houston.

MURDER & MAYHEM
IN
HOUSTON

HISTORIC BAYOU CITY CRIME

MIKE VANCE & JOHN NOVA LOMAX

THE
History
PRESS

Published by The History Press
Charleston, SC 29403
www.historypress.net

Copyright © 2014 by Mike Vance and John Nova Lomax
All rights reserved

First published 2014

Manufactured in the United States

ISBN 978.1.62619.521.9

Library of Congress CIP data applied for.

CONTENTS

PREFACE

It must be said at the outset that this book was never intended to be encyclopedic. We knew of all the later cases, having lived through the Houston media coverage, but with the nineteenth-century stories, one case often led to another. In the end, we found that we could fill three or four of these books with stories that are just as interesting.

Some of the cases contained within may strike you as sadder than others. Some are definitely more brutal. Some may hit a particular chord that is close to home. They are all crimes and tragedies, and we tell them here in the interest of history.

We made every effort to spotlight stories that have slipped into the recesses of this city's gargantuan memory hole. Each new generation tends to forget the history of the one that preceded it here. Maybe that's common to all cities. Maybe New Yorkers, Chicagoans and San Franciscans forget just as swiftly as Houstonians. But the older we get, it seems more astonishing how little the younger Houstonians know about what happened here when we were children or young men in the 1970s and '80s.

We considered some stories too high profile to rehash, including Andrea Yates, the Cheerleader Mom, Coral Eugene Watts, Clara Harris, the Peña-Ertman gang initiation murders and the *Blood and Money* Robinson-Hill killings. Others, such as Dean Corll and Karla Faye Tucker, have been covered elsewhere, but we touch on them here, as they relate to other stories we wanted to tell. In short, if there was already a book or movie about something, then what was the point of retelling it in our few pages?

There are many particularly ghastly cases that we didn't delve into: the 1973 Willow Meadows spree-killing of several little girls who were gunned down as they walked home from school and the brutal 1983 slaying of the Malibu Grand Prix workers come to mind.

We did try to include stories that were linked somehow to others, and it is amazing and chilling to find how many were. In some cases, it's our belief that these tales have never been told in full, or at least not in a prominent enough venue.

Local histories have tended to gloss over this city's dark side, choosing instead to cite the ever-increasing tonnage coming and going from the Houston Ship Channel, the scientific wonders of NASA and the Texas Medical Center, the financial feats of powerful banker-developers like Jesse Jones and the gargantuan deeds of the great oil men.

That's important history to record, but that's only half of Houston's story. It's high time the dark side comes to light. Contrast is the key to any great portrait.

Finally, there is this belief: Houston and New Orleans stand alone as the creepiest cities on the Gulf Coast. With its pervasive voodoo ambience, sprawling cities of the dead, air of genteel decay and long history of murder and mayhem, New Orleans is undeniably a spooky town. Fright is a cottage industry there. Having said that, Houston is not far behind. Houstonians just don't celebrate death and the past the way New Orleanians do. In fact, we tend to simply forget all the awful and weird things that have happened here over the last 179 years or so, and mercifully so because there have been an enormous number of terrible episodes. It's just that with few exceptions, this absent-minded behemoth of a city has forgotten its most chilling outrages, its many midnights in dozens of evil gardens.

ACKNOWLEDGEMENTS

No book happens without plenty of help. We'd like to thank those who are deserving of our sincere gratitude. Several people were interviewed for the various stories. Dr. Stephen Hardin, author of the erudite and entertaining book *Texian Macabre*, was great. Thanks also to Sherrie Tatum and Jeff Statton, who spoke so freely about their painful memories. There were the Cooley family, Bill Thomas, Vic Driscoll, Scott Vogel and four Chambers County experts: Bobby Scherer, Kevin Ladd, Robert Schaadt and Gary Wiggins.

We could not have written much of anything without the Harris County Archives and Sarah Jackson and Annie Golden. The other such magical place is the Houston Metropolitan Research Center of the Houston Public Library. Jo, Laney, Caroline and Aaron were there to help with materials, and Joel Draut and Tim Ronk helped with several images. Lastly, Francisco Heredia of the Harris County District Clerk's Historical Records was terrifically helpful in locating some old files.

Other image help was provided by Jene Anderson of TDCJ Archives in Austin and John Slate of Dallas Municipal Archives. Major Debra Schmidt of the Harris County Sheriff's Department and James Chapman of the Houston Police Department were also generous with their resources. Thanks also to Michael Bailey and Jamie Murray at the Brazoria County History Museum.

A special thank-you goes to some folks such as Margaret Downing, Louis Aulbach and Paul Scott. Christen Thompson of The History Press has graciously walked us through the entire process. Then, last but not least, as they say, huge thanks go to our respective wives, Kelly Graml Lomax and Anne Vance, who had to listen to us ramble on about all this stuff for the last year.

1
ROWDY BEGINNINGS

For the not-yet-two-year-old town of Houston, March 28, 1838, was a banner day—fine weather and the biggest spectacle the capital of Texas had yet seen. On that date, in what was Houston's first widely publicized execution, two convicted murderers were slated to hang simultaneously from a gallows erected near what is now the corner of Main Street and Webster Avenue.[1] A crowd of two to three thousand men, women and children flocked to the hanging tree, where they watched and jeered as David James Jones and John Christopher Columbus Quick were wheeled in a cart under the beam, had ropes placed around their necks and said their last words. Seconds later, the hangman cracked his whip on the team, and the cart was wheeled out from under the doomed men.

Quick met his end after reportedly killing his fifth man. This was Jones' third murder. Unfortunately, in killing a gentleman, Jones chose his victim poorly. Like Quick, Jones was from what was known at the time as the "rowdy loafer" set. The rowdy loafers were impoverished, illiterate, Bowie knife–toting, underemployed, tobacco-spitting backwoods desperadoes in search of adventure, easy money and whiskey-fueled good times. They ranked just above slaves and Mexican servants on the social totem pole of early Houston and far beneath the social elite: the planters, the attorneys, the physicians and the like.[2]

Like many others of their sort, Quick and Jones were combat-tested veterans of the recent war against Santa Anna, and they had hair-trigger tempers. Historian Stephen Hardin writes that a sure way to set them off was to offer them a chance to detect a snub against their honor. "You think you're better 'n me?" was often the last thing said before knives were drawn. As the case of Quick showed, such killings, so long as they were kept among themselves, were almost never prosecuted. "If two rowdy loafers knifed each other up, they certainly weren't going to waste taxpayer money on that," says Hardin. "Good riddance." But when Jones killed above his station, that was another matter.[3]

Life was as cheap as border-town Chiclets in 1830s Houston, a town that made Deadwood look like Zurich by comparison. A visitor from Nacogdoches called what was then the capital of the Republic of Texas "the most miserable place in the world." There was the heat and humidity, unalleviated by air conditioning. Among a host of other maladies, yellow fever alone carried off early Houstonians by the hundreds, their bodies sometimes simply dumped in the muddy, waste-filled streets, where they vied for space with the corpses of dogs, cats, pigs, cattle and horses. A local complained that the stench came "so near as to impregnate the air with its putridity."[4]

All that rotting flesh attracted billions of flies. Fleas "were as thick as the sands of the sea," and Buffalo Bayou was the mosquito's perfect breeding habitat. Just outside town—which was then bounded by Buffalo Bayou,

Original Plan of Houston. From the Mike Vance collection.

Texas Avenue, Crawford Street and Louisiana Street—wolves and panthers howled and caterwauled through the long nights. The miserable shanties almost every Houstonian called home were plagued by rats "almost as large as prairie dogs." People feared sleep because these gargantuan rodents were known to gnaw off toes, fingers and noses.[5]

Catering to the desires of the rowdy loafers, Houston soon bloomed so many gambling houses, grog shops and bordellos that in 1838, one respectable resident declared that Houston was "the greatest sink of disipation [sic] and vice that modern times have known...What a den of villains must there be here?"[6]

Davy Jones was one such villain, albeit one with a more impressive war record than most of his fellows. One of just twenty-eight survivors of the Goliad massacre, Jones made it back to Texan lines in time to fight alongside Sam Houston at San Jacinto.

That patriotic pedigree came to naught, however, when, as the result of a tragic misunderstanding over a horse, Jones stuck his Bowie knife in the guts of a gentleman named Mandred Wood, whose brother Fernando was a future mayor of New York City and whose other brother, Benjamin, later rose to become editor of the *New York Daily News* and a New York state representative.

City fathers knew that this murder was bad for business. If ever Houston was going to rise from the wicked muck, the likes of Davy Jones could not go around stabbing gentlemen like Mandred Wood. "I was flabbergasted that Houston was as brazen and depraved as it was," Hardin says. "But at the same time, you had an upper crust who had a vision for the place that went beyond what they could see out their window every day."[7]

Thus Jones, veteran or not, would have to hang. One-armed Dr. Francis Moore would see to it personally, and as both outspoken mayor and bluenosed editor of the newspaper, he was uniquely positioned to effect just such a result. Try to imagine it in today's Houston: the mayor editorializes in favor of hanging a notorious criminal in her own newspaper and then presides over the execution.

After they were cut down and buried in shallow graves that were practically under the spot where they had swung, Quick and Jones would not slumber long in peace. According to the diary of attorney John Hunter Herndon, later that day five of the town's leading citizens exhumed the corpses, sawed off the heads and retired to Herndon's lodgings to study the shapes of the two skulls for signs of bad character. A day later, the men popped open the skullcaps to sift through the brains, and Herndon decided to keep

Francis Moore Jr., Houston's early law and order mayor. *From the Houston Metropolitan Research Center, Houston Public Library.*

Jones' noggin, which showed bumps indicating great moral deficiency, as a souvenir.

This was the pseudoscience of phrenology in action, and Hardin believes such practices were more common than we might think. "Most people did not record those shenanigans in their diary," he says. "We're just so lucky that he kept that diary and that it survived." Another of Herndon's skull-related entries is even more ghoulish: While on a tear in Galveston, Herndon's friend Dr. Robert Watson guzzled whiskey from a skull "that yet had brains in it."[8]

While that was a little beyond the pale, Herndon apparently saw nothing amiss with keeping two rotting heads in his room for days. He recorded that after pickling Jones' brain, he sat down and cranked out an article for the *Telegraph*, called on one young lady and wrote a love poem to another.

The next day, Herndon visited two associates, curled up with a good book in the late morning and then went for a ride in the country before flirting with more young ladies. After that, it was off "over the prairie beautifully clad with grass and wild flowers" to a Mrs. Smith's, "where we had an excellent supper and fine society." Herndon was back in town by 8:00 p.m., he recorded. "Had several calls," he wrote, before closing out his affairs of the day: "Buried the remains of Quick's and Jones' heads."[9]

The crania were no doubt quite "ripe" by then—a full three days after the hanging. Hardin also believes that Herndon did not reunite the heads with the rest of the bodies.

"Most likely," he wrote, "he traipsed out behind Floyd's Hotel, dug a hole and plunked them in. In morose moments, one wonders if the skulls are still there, forlorn, forgotten, shrouded under the blacktop of a frenzied, modern city."[10]

SUICIDES

Early Houston was not the easiest place to live, even for the successful. Between 1838 and 1858, no fewer than five of the most prominent politicians in Texas committed suicide. Three of the men shot themselves, another leaped (or possibly fell) off a steamboat in Galveston Bay and one gutted himself with a Bowie knife. All called Houston home, at least for a time.

This melancholy tale begins with the Republic of Texas presidential election of 1838. Sam Houston was term-limited out after his two-year term, so the race pitted his arch-nemesis, Mirabeau Lamar, against two candidates who were more to the Big Drunk's liking.

First, there was Peter Grayson. A Virginia-bred lawyer, Grayson was up for consideration by Houston as Texas' consul to the United Kingdom, but when another man got the post, Grayson went on a tear in downtown Houston, where he was spotted roaming "the streets half of one night, drunk, and hatless, coatless, bootless, daring anyone to fight with him."

Evidently behavior like that was not considered political suicide at the time because Grayson soon became Texas attorney general and minister plenipotentiary to the United States. After that, he became Houston's handpicked choice as his would-be successor.

Grayson was a reluctant candidate and regretted his choice to accept the nod almost immediately. He was already blue over a failed marriage proposal and had been dogged by paralyzing fits of depression and madness all his life. The Lamar presidential juggernaut helped push him over the edge—they found out that he had a ne'er-do-well cousin of the same name who had abandoned his family in Kentucky and had pinned that Peter Grayson's sins on him, at least until the Texas Peter Grayson, then fifty years old, could get back home and clear his name.

On July 9, 1838, while returning from an official trip to Washington, Grayson checked into an inn in the Smoky Mountain hamlet of Bean's Station, Tennessee. Witnesses heard him muttering about "fiends" having taken control of his mind before he entered his room, and then they heard a single shot from his pistol. Grayson's worries were over.[11]

Even with all his troubles, Grayson's suicide shocked Anson Jones, the last Texas president and an eventual suicide himself. "I shall be surprised at no ones [sic] committing suicide after hearing of Col. Grayson doing so," he wrote. "It has shocked me more than the Death of a Dozen others."

That left James Collinsworth as Lamar's sole remaining prominent electoral foe, but even as Grayson breathed his last, Collinsworth was five days into a weeklong Fourth of July whiskey bender in Galveston that would end his young life.

Collinsworth and Houston were both lawyers and fellow Tennesseans, and Collinsworth had nominated the Raven as leader of the Texan army back in the revolution days. Houston repaid him by tapping him first as one of his aides-de-camp at the Battle of San Jacinto and later as the chief justice of the Texas Supreme Court. Collinsworth reportedly had a quick temper and once narrowly averted a duel with Anson Jones.

Like Houston, Collinsworth was overly fond of sour mash whiskey, but that was no obstacle to his running for president of the wild-and-woolly Texas of 1838.

Collinsworth headed down to Galveston to campaign and party, and it appears the holiday got the best of him. The Fourth was one of the days on which it was culturally acceptable for men of his stature to be drunk in public—indeed, it was almost expected. However, Collinsworth could not cork the jug on the fifth. Or the next day. Or on the seventh, eighth, ninth or tenth either. And on the eleventh, while aboard a steamboat in Galveston Bay, Collinsworth jumped (or fell) into the waves and drowned.[12]

Jones was not surprised by Collinsworth's manner of demise. He would later say he "expected it (of Collinsworth) as I knew him to be deranged and when excited by liquor, almost mad."

With his two main rivals dead of suicides within two days of each other, Lamar won the election in a walk and moved the capital of Texas from Houston to Austin.

Like both Sam Houston and James Collinsworth, George Campbell Childress was a Nashville lawyer and, like Houston, was tied in with President Andrew Jackson's Scots-Irish McMafia. Unlike Houston and Collinsworth, the baby-faced Childress was not a drinker. Childress was also a newspaper editor, and using his journalistic and legal skills, it was he who drafted the Texas Declaration of Independence in 1836. After the revolution, the widowed Childress returned to Nashville, practiced law and remarried, in hopes of one day bringing his new bride to Texas with him. Childress spent the next several years hanging out his shingle in Houston, Galveston and Nashville and failing every time.

In October 1841, Childress was at the end of his rope. The thirty-seven-year-old was living in Mrs. Crittenden's boardinghouse in Galveston. President Lamar had refused his plaintive entreaty for a government job. His brother had gambled away his pitiful nest egg. He was eight hundred miles from his wife and children. He sat down with pen and paper and wrote

The troubled George Childress, author of the Texas Declaration of Independence. *From the Mike Vance collection.*

letters back home settling his affairs, walked across the hall to Mrs. Crittenden's room and pounded on the door. He begged his landlady to save him from himself, then unsheathed his Bowie knife and stabbed himself in the guts six times, spattering the poor Mrs. Crittenden with blood.

Childress died three hours later, most of which time he spent futilely begging for a clergyman to come baptize him. The author of the Texas Declaration of Independence was buried in an unmarked grave. It's believed to be under the playground of Rosenberg School at 721 10th Street; a cenotaph in Galveston's Episcopal Cemetery was erected in 1935 and does not mark his resting place.[13]

By 1857, South Carolina native and longtime Nacogdoches planter Thomas Jefferson Rusk had held just about every high office in Texas, from secretary of war back in the Republic days to chief justice of the Texas Supreme Court to United States senator and president pro tem of the Senate. Regarded by some party bigwigs as presidential timber in both Texas and the United States, Rusk always shied away from running.

He would have seemed to have it all, and yet he had nothing, for in the spring of 1856, his beloved wife, Polly, died of tuberculosis, leaving him with the care of five of their seven children, two others having reached adulthood.

Rusk was less chauvinistic than many of the men of his time and went out of his way to praise women.

"The men of Texas deserved much credit, but more was due the women," he once said. "Armed men facing a foe could not but be brave; but the women, with their little children around them, without means of defense or power to resist, faced danger and death with unflinching courage."

The much-decorated Thomas Rusk, hero of Texas and suicide victim. *From the Mike Vance collection.*

Already despondent over Polly's death, wracked by guilt for choosing his career over his children and facing his own grim medical prognosis after a tumor had been found at the base of his neck, Rusk told his family he was going squirrel hunting one day and walked out the door with a musket. He apparently rigged the trigger with a string and managed to shoot himself in the head. Sam Houston broke the news to the United States Senate, and members honored Rusk by wearing black crepe for the next thirty days.[14]

The final member of this quintet of talented, terminally depressive men is Dr. Anson Jones, a man who had noted the deaths of the others in his own diary.

Born into poverty in Great Barrington, Massachusetts, in 1798, Jones trained as a physician in New York State and failed to establish a medical practice in Philadelphia, where he was jailed briefly for debt.

Dr. Jones headed for the sunny south—all the way to Venezuela, where he evidently made some money. In 1832, he resurfaced stateside in New Orleans. There, he abandoned medicine and became a businessman. He also contracted yellow fever, gambled recklessly and, in his own words, found himself "learning to imitate the fashionable practice of taking a 'julep' much oftener than was at all necessary." He swiftly went broke. Again.

The following year found him practicing medicine again, this time in Brazoria, Mexican Texas. Here his medical practice finally thrived.

During the war, Jones served the Texas army as a judge advocate and surgeon, though he humble-braggingly insisted on holding a lowly private's rank. After the war, Jones returned to Brazoria, where he found a squatter practicing law from his clinic—none other than the soon-to-be-drowned James Collinsworth. Jones evicted the hotheaded Tennessean from his office, and friends headed off the duel that was looming between the two men.

Jones then entered politics and served as the Republic's secretary of state and eventually became the last president of the Republic of Texas. In Austin, on February 19, 1846, Jones struck the Lone Star flag from atop the flagpole on the capitol grounds for the last time and handed it to a weeping Sam Houston.

Jones hoped to become a senator but was passed over time and time again, and the perceived slight festered in his soul as the years rolled on. Houston, whom Jones had come to despise, and Rusk were the first to beat him out. He took to moping, once reportedly writing to a friend that he would never be elected, that an uncaring public had forgotten all the good he had done for it and that he had been forgotten, "just as they forgot Grayson."

Even as his wife and children adored him and Barrington (his Brazoria County plantation) thrived, Jones' funk continued. And yet hope was born anew. In 1857, he saw one last chance. Both Senate seats were coming open. Houston was running for governor, and Rusk had just shot himself.

Jones traveled to Austin and expected a coronation from a grateful legislature, but instead he received exactly zero votes from that august body.

A devastated Dr. Jones rashly sold his plantation at a quarter of its value and decided to settle for opening a medical practice in Galveston.

Anson Jones, the last president of the Republic of Texas. *From the Mike Vance collection.*

While making those arrangements, he chose to come to Houston for a few days. Here, he wallowed in misery and regret in the Old Capitol Hotel, the same building in which he had served as a congressman as a young man. Back then, all things seemed possible and the future limitless, but now he was weeks away from his sixtieth birthday and doomed to spend out his days as a humble doctor.

On the night of January 8, Jones and a friend sat up late in his room. "My public career began in this house, and I have been thinking it might close here," Jones reportedly told his friend. The friend left at 2:00 a.m. on

January 9. An hour later, Dr. Jones made good on his promise by taking out his pistol and shooting himself in the head.

Even his epitaph was bitter:

> *The echo of his words lingers in the*
> *Councils of his Country, alone unheard by*
> *ears deaf to the claims of merit, dull to*
> *the voice of Honor and dead to the calls*
> *of Justice;*
> *To them the sand*
> *To Thee the Marble!*[15]

THE MURDER OF JACK VANCE

Obedience Fort Smith's name appears to this day on the deeds for billions of dollars' worth of property in Midtown Houston. The Republic of Texas survey bearing her name granted her 3,368 acres just outside the fledgling city. Her eleven children were as fruitful as their mother, and several of their offspring earned an honorable place in Texas history.

Her last two boys, twins David Andrew Jackson Smith and Elias William Shelby Smith, were not such overachievers. Arriving in Mexican Texas prior to the revolution, Jackson Smith had established a Houston law practice with Platt Crosby, a man soon to be his father-in-law, by late 1837. Their offices were in Floyd's Hotel, the same establishment that was home to John Hunter Herndon. In fact, it was Jackson Smith who befriended Herndon and invited him "to take part of his room and bed."[16] Weeks later, Herndon would help celebrate Jackson Smith's wedding.

Jackson's twin brother, Shelby, was a sport. For starters, he loved his dog. When someone absconded with the animal, Shelby ran ads in the local paper for two months.

> *Thirty Dollars Reward. Stolen from the subscriber, near Houston, a small dusky white BULL DOG, very low, heavy built; his under teeth very perceptible; large head. The dog was taken out of town two months since. The above reward will be given for the dog, or fifty for the thief with the dog. Shelby Smith.*[17]

The animals that Shelby Smith loved even more than dogs, however, were his horses. Blooded racehorses, to be precise.

There was no diversion, sport or entertainment in early Houston that could hold a candle to horse racing. President Sam Houston himself owned several racehorses, sometimes sending notice to his wife, Margaret, to have one or the other brought to the town of Houston. Some of these Thoroughbreds cost the Raven upwards of $5,000.[18]

Nobody in town, however, was more involved in the horse races than young Shelby Smith. He was a charter member of the Houston Jockey Club, formed in 1838 with a meeting at Kesler's Arcade Saloon.[19] Smith was one of five on the rules committee that voted to largely adopt the regulations of the Metairie Jockey Club of New Orleans. He was also one of the few Jockey Club founders who couldn't claim a Texas army officer's rank before his name. Robert Barr, the postmaster general of the Republic, was jockey club president.[20]

They set up the Post Oak Course, located on sixty acres belonging to club member L.C. Stanley and situated near the modern-day intersection of Montrose Boulevard and West Dallas Street. President Houston owned his own ranch and racing field just to the east of Stanley's tract. They also used a course near Spring Creek.

Shelby Smith owned several horses of good lineage, and he raced them over distances of one to four miles. The prizes and costs were considerable. Purses were several hundred dollars each, and that didn't include the considerable side betting that at least one observer reported to be as high as $2,500 on one race. The fall meet of 1839 bore an entrance fee of $500, and Smith's mare, Charlotte Hill, won the top purse in what the newspaper called a "beautiful race."[21]

Dr. Ashbel Smith, pioneering physician, educator and diplomat of early Texas, wrote that there was "a larger proportion of well bred geldings about Houston than I have seen in any other part of the world. The days of the races were concluded by a ball given by the Club. It was a large assembly of elegant ladies and high bred gentlemen; the festivities of the night were unmarred by any adverse incident."[22]

Given the preponderance of idleness, alcohol and honor in the town, such an adverse incident was inevitable. It came in April 1840 when Shelby Smith shot and killed a fellow horse owner named John S. "Jack" Vance at the races in Houston. Vance's and Smith's horses had been running against each other for at least a year, so it was possible that a feud had been simmering.[23]

The *Brazos Courier*, a newspaper in Brazoria, Texas, reported on San Jacinto Day, "We learn that in a rencountre at the Houston races a few days ago, a man named Vance, (a gambler) was shot by Shelby Smith. Vance expired immediately." Another Texas news story a few weeks later named both of the Smith twins going against Vance and a seriously injured Mr. Patterson. Francis Moore Jr. of Houston's *Telegraph and Texas Register*, a shameless booster of the city, did not run the story.[24]

German diarist Gustav Dresel almost certainly wrote of the incident, though the accepted translation into English lists the perpetrator as "a wealthy planter Walker." The original of Dresel's diary is thought to be lost, and the several handwritten copies that do exist (all in German) each have differences, minor or major. It is rather easy to mark the confusion over the name to the several years that elapsed between the incident in Houston and someone else making copies of a copy in Germany. It is next to impossible not to square the transcription of Dresel's report below with the newspaper articles and the existing court records:

> *Horse races were frequent and gave rise to scenes that characterize the social life of that time in Texas. Once the wealthy planter Walker made a bet with the gambler Vance, the stakes being the horses on which they were mounted. Walker Lost. He contested the bet. A dispute ensued. Walker shot a bullet through Vance's heart. The latter's few friends drew their pistols and in a few minutes seven of the shooters were more or less seriously wounded. Walker was arrested and indicted by the district attorney for murder, but set free under five thousand-dollar bond.[25]*

Charges for the murder of Jack Vance were quickly handed down against the twins, Shelby and Jackson Smith, as well as their nineteen-year-old nephew, Frank Terry, who would find both his fame and demise during the Civil War as commander of Terry's Texas Rangers.

Two days later, charges against Terry were deemed not worthy of pursuing, and the indictment against the brothers changed to assault with intent to kill. Bonds were high, set initially at $10,000 plus $5,000 securities but then raised to $15,000 each with an additional $10,000 each in securities. The men posting this money included their older brother and well-known saloonkeeper, Ben Fort Smith, along with Ashbel Smith and Francis Lubbock, a Houston businessman and future Civil War governor of Texas.

The bulk of the court records are missing, so following the events in detail is difficult, but it appears that the case was somehow dropped since on December 19, 1840, a true bill of murder came from a different grand jury. This indictment restored all three original defendants. A jury pool of thirty-six "good and lawful" men was seated, but when the trial began on December 23, only Shelby Smith was in the dock. A day later, on Christmas Eve, the jury rendered a verdict of not guilty "without retiring from their box." It again jibes with the conclusion of Dresel's diary entry: "But since Vance had no lawyer to represent him, the matter was dropped."[26]

With the lack of certain details, it is impossible to say definitively, but it is difficult to ignore the contrast between Jones and Quick, rowdy loafers hanged for killing a society man, and Shelby Smith, a society man acquitted of killing a gambler. Such was early Houston.

2
CIVIL WAR AND RECONSTRUCTION

HONOR AND DISHONOR

Any suffering in Houston during the Civil War came largely at the hands of Federal gunboats that were blockading Galveston. Cotton planters had slowed shipping through the city due to fear that their bales would be seized and burned by the United States troops. With the flow of goods from the sea dried up in both directions, locals faced certain hardships. Complaints were heard that retailers marked up dry goods more than 500 percent, even on merchandise they had purchased at pre-blockade prices. Shoes and boots tripled in price. Flour ran as high as two dollars per pound and eggs four bucks a dozen.[27] Houstonians drank brews of dried okra or sweet potatoes in lieu of coffee, which was almost impossible to find. British journalist Arthur Freemantle, passing through Texas, noted that the substitutes were "not generally very successful."[28] The newspapers kept printing, but sometimes the editions came out on brown wrapping paper or even on the backside of patterned wallpaper. Still, the relative lack of Federal ground forces and the proximity to Mexico left Texas better off than other rebellious states.

It also helped that Houston was generally swimming with Confederate officers. Texas was part of the Department of Trans-Mississippi, which had an important headquarters in the Bayou City to oversee the District of Texas, New Mexico and Arizona. When fifty-five-year-old John Bankhead Magruder arrived in Houston in November 1862 as the new top man in the district, the populace was thrilled. Magruder had a long and storied career in the United States Army, but the stories included not only unquestioned courage and decision making in battle but also a penchant for heavy drinking and outrageously flamboyant uniforms. Dubbed "Prince John," he had graduated from West Point and also attended the University of Virginia, where a classmate was Edgar Allan Poe. He had a buoyant personality and loved putting on plays cast with members of the officer corps. What thrilled the locals, however, was that Magruder understood the value of the area. In a comment to warm a Lone Star heart, he stated that Texas was the only part of the department that mattered and that "whoever is the master of the railroads of Houston and Galveston is the master of Texas."[29]

There were plenty of gray-clad soldiers coming and going around Houston, too. The vast majority of the ninety-two thousand or so white males in the 1860 United States Census of Texas saw some form of military service for the Confederate cause. Of those, more than two-thirds spent the war in Texas or a neighboring state or territory, famous exceptions such as Hood's Texas Brigade and Terry's Texas Rangers notwithstanding.[30]

One regiment that recruited heavily in the Houston area was commanded by John S. "Rip" Ford, the legendary Texas Ranger. Ford's men spent the war battling Comanches, Union troops and Juan Cortina's Mexican raiders. In midsummer of 1861, four companies of Ford's cavalry headed to far West Texas under the leadership of John Robert Baylor with an eye on invading New Mexico and claiming it for the Confederacy. They moved about forty miles upstream from El Paso and took the hamlet of Mesilla without much of a fight. After forcing the surrender of a United States Army detail at Fort Fillmore, just across the Rio Grande, Baylor proclaimed that the CSA now owned the Confederate Territory of Arizona and decreed that he, John R. Baylor, was governor. The ensuing campaign was less successful than the capture of Mesilla, and though they styled themselves the Arizona Brigade, Baylor's men spent the war in Texas, never seeing modern-day Arizona.

Some years before, teenaged John Baylor and his family had moved to Fort Gibson, Indian Territory, when his father, an army surgeon, was stationed there. By his eighteenth birthday, he was near La Grange, Texas, living with his uncle and fighting Comanches on the new Republic's frontier. He returned to Indian Territory only to be accused of murder, perhaps unjustly, when a friend's fight turned deadly. Forced to flee, he was soon back in Texas with a wife and a future in politics. Much of his focus was still on what he saw as duplicitous Comanches, and he soon formed a vigilante group and went off to fight Indians, a pastime that occupied him until Texas secession and war.[31]

George Wythe Baylor later in life, after his Confederate military career. *From the Western History Collection, University of Oklahoma Libraries.*

By the time of his reinvention as territorial governor, his officer corps in West Texas included George Wythe Baylor, John R.'s younger brother. The two brothers were close. After an unfulfilling trip to the gold fields of California, George moved in with John in Weatherford, Texas, in 1859. A year later, George told the census taker that his occupation was that of "Indian Killer," a badge earned when he took nine scalps while accompanying his older sibling on a raid at Paint Creek. In fact, an all-consuming hatred of the American Indians was a bond that the two Baylors would share throughout their lives.[32]

While in Mesilla in 1861, John Baylor, who had published a prewar newspaper called the *White Man*, issued an order to his troops that they should use "all means to persuade the Apaches or any tribe to come in for the purpose of making peace, and when you get them together kill all the grown Indians and take the children prisoners and sell them to defray the expense of killing the adult Indians." Though there is no record of these extermination orders being carried out, the brutality of it didn't sit well with his Confederate superiors, who relieved the governor of his duty and his officer's commission.

It was also in Mesilla that Governor John Baylor shot to death Robert Kelly, a local newspaper editor who had been repeatedly critical of him in print. Upon encountering the scribe in a local store, the two quarreled, and it turned out that Kelly quite literally had brought a knife to gunfight. The chronicler leaving the most detailed record of the episode was his young brother, George Wythe Baylor.

George W. Baylor's immediate fortunes were notably better than his older brother's. He left West Texas to take a posting as senior aide-de-camp to General Albert Sidney Johnston, the top-ranking Texan in Confederate service. Unfortunately for George, Johnston was killed at Shiloh in April 1862, and Baylor was on the move back to Texas. He became a cavalry colonel once again in the Arizona Brigade, fought in the Red River campaign and was cited for gallantry at the Battles of Malvern Hill and Pleasant Hill.

For all of Baylor's Texas pioneer credentials, John Austin Wharton was pure-D Texas royalty. His father, William Harris Wharton, would easily rank in the top five on a list of men who pushed hardest to start the Texas Revolution. His namesake uncle was no slouch in that department either. His mother was the only daughter of Jared Groce, the richest of Stephen Austin's Old Three Hundred. To add to the legacy, Wharton went away to college in South Carolina and returned married to the governor's daughter. He studied law with a South Carolina senator and a future governor of Texas, established a law partnership of his own and lived on his Brazoria County plantation, served by at least 135 slaves.[33]

When the Civil War broke out, Wharton entered as a captain in the famed Eighth Texas Cavalry, known as Terry's Texas Rangers, commanded by his cousin, Frank Terry. The battlefield deaths of Terry and his immediate subordinate elevated Wharton to command of the unit. He distinguished himself before being severely wounded at Shiloh, was wounded again at Murfreesboro, led a brilliant charge at Bardstown and earned yet more glory at Chickamauga. It all added up to a fast rise up the ladder of command. At the age of thirty-six, John Austin Wharton earned the stars of a Confederate major general. On top of his wealth and family, Wharton could add an impeccable résumé of his own.[34]

As the war in the East slowly ground toward an inevitable Union victory, some Rebel leaders felt that successes could be found in the Trans-Mississippi, and Wharton was transferred back to his home state. It was an assignment popular with the Lone Star elite. By the spring of 1865, newspapers from around the state were suggesting that John Austin Wharton was a front-runner to be the next governor of Texas.[35]

Despite later testimony to the contrary, there had been no love lost between George Baylor and John Wharton for some time. Some difficulty dated to casualties sustained by Baylor's troops in Arkansas at least a year prior. He placed the blame for the losses on Wharton. Soon after, Baylor had asked for leave to visit his sick wife, only to have Wharton note on the request that he was unfamiliar with the circumstances. Wharton viewed Baylor as a less than "good and useful officer." The final straw

John Austin Wharton, heir to a blue-blood Texas legacy. *From the Brazoria County History Museum.*

for Baylor came when Wharton reorganized the Southeast Texas command structure, dismounting his cavalry and placing Baylor underneath David S. Terry, another of Wharton's cousins and a colonel with less seniority. Moreover, Baylor had quarrels with David Terry that dated back to his California Gold Rush days.[36]

Baylor even drew a stern dinner table remonstrance from his wife in mid-March 1865 for asserting that, if given half a chance, he would kill Wharton himself. General Wharton had a reputation for being unfailingly loyal to his friends or cliquish and dictatorial, depending on where one stood. Clearly Baylor was standing on the outside.[37]

On the morning of April 6, 1865, George W. Baylor, accompanied by Captain Richard Henry Douglas Sorrel of his company, walked to Central Depot just north of Buffalo Bayou because Baylor wished to speak with newly minted brigadier general Walter P. Lane. Somewhere on the way back, they happened upon General Wharton riding in a buggy with General James E. Harrison. Sorrel, at least, saluted.

Wharton "hailed Colonel Baylor and said, 'Colonel, you are needed at your command.'" That brought the six-foot, two-inch Baylor to the side of the open buggy. Baylor, knowing he was in Houston without leave, asserted that he had to stay in town to keep his men from deserting.

"Have any deserted?" asked Wharton.

"No, but they will if I am compelled to obey the order forcing me to report to a junior colonel," was Baylor's retort. He continued to rant, telling Wharton that he had been "imposed upon by you, General." At one point, even his friend and subordinate, Sorrel, admitted that Baylor "raised his hand toward General Wharton as if to take hold of him, but did not." Harrison, holding the reins, testified that Baylor "struck at Wharton."

Sorrel and another witness asserted that Wharton called Baylor a "damned liar." Harrison said it was Baylor who called Wharton a "liar and a demagogue." All parties agree that General Harrison kept trying to urge the horses forward, away from the very public confrontation.

As the argument grew more vocal and excited, General Wharton ordered that Colonel Baylor consider himself under arrest and leave the city immediately to join his unit near Hempstead. He was to take the same train that Wharton and Harrison were on their way to board. Baylor responded that he would talk to General Magruder first and that he would have justice, adding that though Wharton outranked him now, "there was a day coming when they would be on equal footing."

Baylor headed for General Magruder's headquarters, located in the Fannin House Hotel on Fannin Street and Congress Avenue. Though he asserted that he saw no indications of imminent trouble, Captain Sorrel went next door and committed the events of the morning to paper.[38]

Magruder, just back from breakfast, received Colonel Baylor, who was so beside himself that he was in tears. The district commander led his weeping subordinate to a private room upstairs and told him to compose himself.[39]

While seated on their train and awaiting departure, Generals Wharton and Harrison determined to postpone their own trip to their commands at Hempstead in order to speak to Magruder. They arrived at Fannin House shortly after Baylor. Wharton was seeking to ensure that his arrest of Colonel Baylor was indeed known to General Magruder. Finding the door to the district commander's office locked, Wharton went through another door where Colonel Baylor was still sitting on the side of the bed. Upon entering, Wharton accused Baylor of having "insulted him most grossly." Fearing trouble, General Harrison hurried to get between them.

John Wharton, a somewhat smallish, unathletic man, clenched his fist and was shaking it in George Baylor's face. The two men were again shouting at each other. As Harrison sought to push Wharton back, Baylor, without ever rising from his seated position, drew an ivory-handled Navy Colt pistol on the unarmed generals, reached between Harrison's arm and body to stick the gun next to Wharton's ribs and fired. John Wharton doubled over, hand to his breast and blood coming from his mouth. He managed to choke out the word "Oh" twice before he sank to the floor and died.[40]

John Austin Wharton received a military funeral with full honors. Prince John Magruder personally led the procession down Main Street. Wharton's body was then handed over to his wife for burial at Hempstead. Baylor, meanwhile, was arrested.

In the few weeks following the murder of General Wharton, the situation in Houston deteriorated greatly. Robbery, plundering and general lawlessness abounded. In Galveston, gangs of boys were stealing army ordnance and firing it off. Though Robert E. Lee had signed a surrender of the largest Confederate army on April 9—only three days after the murder—Texas forces held on. The newspapers in Houston and Galveston scoffed at any notion of the rebellion's end.

In mid-May, Magruder was still talking a good game, vowing to die "rather than submit to a force so base, so grasping."[41] An observer of this speech noted that the soldiers being addressed were silent and much less than enthusiastic. Within two weeks, one soldier stationed in Houston told some Galveston cohorts that his comrades in the Bayou City had "laid down their arms and want to go home, war is over."[42]

When the order to evacuate Galveston was given on May 21, the island's Confederate troops swarmed into Houston. Discipline quickly evaporated. The saloons were ordered closed by Houston's mayor, William Anders, amid rumors that the troops planned to burn the town, but the mostly sober soldiery began sacking the town anyway. All Confederate stores of ordnance and clothing were broken into and carried off. It ended officially on June 2, 1865, when Trans-Mississippi commander Edmund Kirby Smith, a Hempstead native, went aboard a United States gunboat in Galveston Harbor and signed the surrender.[43]

In all the disarray of a dying rebel nation, the trial of George W. Baylor sat rather low on the totem pole. The criminal matter was soon in the civilian justice system, although in those uncertain days filled with vanquished Texans and Yankee occupiers, civil justice was a bit of a moving target. It wasn't until two years later that bringing George W. Baylor to trial truly gained traction in a series of aborted trials.

As the jury deliberated on the night of May 18, 1868, the *Houston Telegraph* seemed to suggest a collective throwing up of hands over an inevitable killing:

It was one of the most distressing and grievous misfortunes of the time… Both were noted as good men, brave men, as soldiers and gentlemen. They became embroiled in an official military difference, became embittered toward each other, a personal collision ensured, and the result was that high-souled Wharton lost his life at the hands of noble-spirited Baylor. It was a public misfortune and a public grief. We never knew a case in which there was at the same time such general sorrow and so little unkind feeling toward either of the parties.[44]

Evidently there were enough men on the panel who felt that shooting an unarmed colleague was less "noble-spirited" than the editor of the *Telegraph* believed. The result was another hung jury.[45]

Harris County prosecutors were nothing if not determined. The case was again brought before the district court in December of the same year. Teams for the prosecution and defense were the same, with the exception of General James E. Harrison having joined Jack Harris to argue for conviction. At the conclusion of witness testimony, an argument arose over whether the charge should be murder or manslaughter. Judge George R. Scott ruled that it was the higher standard of murder. At 3:00 p.m. on Thursday, December 4, 1868, after one and a half days before the court, the charge went to the jury. Jurors deliberated only half an hour before making George Wythe Baylor a free man. Spectators crowded around the colonel, and Baylor's wife shed copious tears of joy.[46]

The main players in the drama went back to their lives. James Harrison returned to his hometown of Waco, and in at least a slight irony, Wharton's staunchest defender became a trustee of Baylor University, the institution founded by George Baylor's cousin. At the collapse of the Confederacy, General John Magruder fled to Mexico, where he served for a time in Emperor Maximilian's army. John Austin Wharton's body was removed from its original burial place and reinterred at the Texas State Cemetery.

Open to move on with his life, George Wythe Baylor returned to West Texas as the commander of a company in the Frontier Battalion of the Texas Rangers. He made his headquarters in Ysleta and set about chasing Apaches, often in cooperation with Mexican authorities, to whom he extended "the privilege of coming over on our side and killing all the reservation Indians." He retired from the Rangers in 1885, beloved by his men but still considered undisciplined. He moved on to serve in the state legislature. Baylor died in San Antonio in 1916. Several times in his later years, he described his killing of John Wharton as a "lifelong sorrow," but he often added that he would do the same thing again under the circumstances.[47]

A BAD TIME TO BE BLACK

Just as in the rest of the conquered South, many longtime Houstonians faced Reconstruction with a mix of war weariness and defiant bitterness. The city was occupied by United States troops in mid-June 1865, and things did not start well. As the Thirty-fourth Iowa Infantry, veterans of Vicksburg, marched into town for the first time, a young black man named William, who had enlisted as a cook in Company K, walked some distance ahead of the main body of troops. He was murdered in the street by "a white man named Cotton."[48]

Texans especially chafed at Republican governor Edmund J. Davis' appointment of black militiamen, who had authority over the ex-Confederates. Ten prominent white citizens of Houston, concerned for their lifestyle, became charter members of a secret white citizens' council, a Ku Klux Klan group, and their membership quickly grew to over three hundred. As late as the 1920s, the surviving members openly bragged about how they saved Texas.[49]

Though their legal rights were greatly expanded on paper, life for African Americans in Southeast Texas was not easy or welcoming in the post–Civil War years. The Black Codes adopted by the state government in 1866 were trumpeted as more liberal than any other ex-Confederate state, but such praise was highly relative to say the least. The new racial equality was written of in the press, but practice was something far different. A traveling circus in Galveston happily admitted both races into the big tent. Tickets for whites were twenty-five cents—for blacks, fifty.[50]

Punishment for blacks in the legal system was harsher, and once in prison, they were viewed as a source of free labor, leased out to white landowners for field work. On the very day that a Galveston paper concluded its coverage of George Baylor's last hung jury, it also reported that "William Teese, a Negro, was convicted this morning of theft committed in stealing a watch and was sent to the penitentiary for two years."[51]

Not surprisingly, many blacks never made it into the justice system at all. The immediate postwar years predated the era of organized public lynchings that were partially viewed as entertainment. In the late 1860s and 1870s, African Americans thought to have offended generally faced their fatal comeuppance on the spot. The Klan and similar organizations operated in secret, and hundreds of deaths were never reported; executions were meted out through the end of a pistol or shotgun barrel.

Often, the whites took greatest offense when a black person would take the newly offered freedom to heart. Cases of this sort were reported to

The Klan in post–Civil War costumes. Many Reconstruction-era Houstonians spoke proudly of their Klan membership even decades later. *From the Library of Congress.*

the Freedmen's Bureau throughout the last half of 1865 and well into 1866. Esom Wood in Montgomery County shot and killed an African American stock tender because the man would not allow Wood to whip him. Colonel Henry M. Elmore of Waverly assembled an armed group of neighbors and a pack of hounds to hunt down a freedman named Slade who wanted to leave. They caught him and imprisoned him in a "calaboose on the plantation." Misters Addison and Beads of Walker County also used hounds to track down Isaac, who had the gall to leave the plantation on which he had been living. Another Montgomery County citizen, Dr. George Phillips, whipped a freedman named Leton and put him on a chain for attempting to leave. Leton was still wearing the chain when he made it to Houston to file his complaint.[52]

Many of the former slaves stayed on their plantations as sharecroppers or even for wages, but that was no guarantee of safety. In early December 1865, a freedman named Oliver traveled from Montgomery County to the Freedmen's Bureau in Houston to file a complaint of unpaid wages against Elisha Uzzell. When he returned to his home, Uzzell's son, Major Uzzell, and Dr. McQueen beat him with sticks and then shot and killed him. Six months later, John January of Harrisburg assaulted a former slave named William with a hatchet in a dispute over wages. William suffered a severe cut to his neck.[53]

The old Houston whites seemed to object just as much to the Yankee interlopers as to the freed slaves who had recently been under their thumb.

Dr. S.O. Young—a physician, *Houston Post* columnist and holder of postwar Houston Klan badge no. 11—had this recollection of Reconstruction Houston:

> *There were returned Confederate soldiers out of employment, tough Federal soldiers, gamblers, cut-throats, thugs and bad men of every description, while worse than all else combined, there were thousands of newly freed, ignorant and idle negroes who were completely under the control of designing carpetbaggers, who were constantly putting them up to something to enrage the white men. Slung-shooting and highway robberies were of almost nightly occurrence, and every man carried his life in his hands and knew that he did so.*

Young had at least a partial point in his frustration over Freedmen's Bureau agents overruling local law enforcement. Stories abounded among the locals of incidents such as one in Houston in which a black man arrested for attempted murder escaped from jail only to have the bureau agent protect him from being rearrested.

The Union men had ample reason to believe that the deck was stacked against accused African Americans, however. In Brenham, two unarmed United States soldiers were shot and wounded. The local grand jury no-billed the shooters but "indicted Major Smith for burglary because he broke into the house of some citizen to arrest these two men."[54]

The difference facing enraged former Confederates was that taking out one's frustrations by killing a Northern white scoundrel was not as easy to get away with as a crime against blacks. For any lawlessness on one side, there was certainly plenty on the opposite side of the equation, too. Just before Christmas 1865, a freedman named Jefferson was cut and robbed on a road about a mile outside Houston. The same attackers struck three other freedmen the same night. They escaped.

The same week, near the town of Montgomery, a white gang was robbing blacks. The victims included one freedman who lost $220, money to be split among his fellow farm hands for selling the two bales of cotton that represented their share of that year's crop. Another gang, or possibly the same one, raided an African American dance near Plantersville, robbing and scattering the merrymakers.[55]

When the tables turned, the white press rejoiced. Houston's *Evening Star* provided a salient example with this entry:

> *Flake's Bulletin reports that one of the agents of the Freedmen's Bureau was unmercifully beaten and robbed of $4,000. What a pity!*[56]

The reasons given to bureau agents by white perpetrators of violence against their new, African American fellow citizens were often downright chilling, especially in deep East Texas between the Neches and the Sabine, where many blacks were still openly held in slavery. Freedmen's Bureau inspector general William E. Strong reported that blacks there were "shot down like wild beasts, without any provocation, followed with hounds and maltreated in every possible way." Justifications included complaints that a freedman wouldn't give up his money fast enough, didn't tip his hat or wouldn't share his whiskey flask. Some killings were done just "to see them kick."[57]

Some acts of violence seemed to have no motive other than racial hatred and cruelty. John C. Robert of Houston set fire to the house of a freedwoman named Celia Lindsay on January 1, 1866, and then stood by to prevent anyone from attempting to extinguish the blaze. In Brazoria County in July 1865, C.C. Millican and W.S. Spencer, men around forty, went on a rampage against some local blacks. They started by dragging a young boy from town, tying him to a tree and giving him "two to three hundred lashes with a heavy leather strap." Three weeks later, they "inflicted several severe blows with the iron butt end of a heavy whip on the head of a mulatto woman named Adelaide, cutting to the bone." Spencer then tied her hands, pulled her dress up and raped her. Their stated reason was that Adelaide had "made an insulting noise" when one of their wives passed. They were turned in to the Freedmen's Bureau by seventy-year-old Joel Spencer, Adelaide's former owner and father one of the perpetrators.[58]

S.O. Young opined that the local police force was the only voice of reason that held any power in Houston, and they had their hands full with the situation. As a case in point, Young noted the mass slaying of a black vigilante mob in 1868. Led by a black preacher, about fifty newly freed African Americans came to the city jail with the intent to remove and lynch another black who committed murder the previous night. The preacher put a pistol to the head of City Marshal I.S. Lord, but it was knocked aside by another party. Two deputy marshals on hand immediately opened fire, and "when the smoke cleared there were several dead negroes on the ground. The preacher escaped for a moment, but was killed by [Deputy Alex] Erichsen a few minutes later." Young recalled the incident approvingly.[59]

The Freedmen's Bureau left Houston in 1868. Gone with the bureau was the most likely place for African American citizens to air their grievances with any hope of someone listening. It would be quite some time before the situation got tangibly better.

3
SWEET REVENGE

Revenge is about as time honored a murder motive as one can find, but the years between Reconstruction and the turn of the nineteenth century were particularly good ones for revenge, however misguided on occasion. To be sure, all of the perpetrators believed they were only doing what had to be done.

Doctor William Pitt Riddell studied at Amherst and Yale before earning his medical degree from the University of Louisiana in New Orleans. In the 1850s, he moved to Houston and was active in the Texas Geological Society and the Masonic Lodge. During the Civil War, Dr. Riddell headed the Bayou City's medical hospital. By 1872, he was forty-three years old and described as a "fine physical specimen" with a wife who was barely thirty and a young daughter. It is safe to say that he was one of the most respected doctors in town.[60]

Thus there was no hesitation when Dr. Riddell was recommended to recently arrived resident Thomas Atkinson as just the man to handle a female complaint for Leona, his wife of one year. Young Mrs. Atkinson saw Riddell several times over three or four months, both in her home and in his office above J.C. Conliff's Drug Store. But during one Monday office visit, things got out of hand.[61]

Mrs. Atkinson was undressed and reclined on the examination couch. Such behavior was required given the nature of her complaint, she said. Riddell, examining "her womb," suddenly said he was tired and "laid his head on (her) breast," commenting, "Oh my God, what a thing it is to be with a pretty woman."

Leona pushed him away but said that he tried unsuccessfully to pull her back onto the couch. The doctor did not push things any further but did entreat her not to say anything, a promise she initially made.

That evening, Mr. Atkinson, a railroad conductor, returned from an out-of-town run aboard a Texas Central freight. After dinner, Mrs. Atkinson asked him to take a walk with her. Along the way, she told him of the events at Dr. Riddell's office. At Mr. Atkinson's insistence, they went to the home of T.P. Robinson, the man who had recommended Riddell in the first place. Robinson assured the couple that he knew nothing of the alleged attack. Atkinson asked to borrow Robinson's pistol. Robinson refused but agreed to serve as a liaison between the impugned doctor and the frantic husband.[62]

Robinson went to see his friend the doctor, though by the time of the inquest testimony, the doctor had been publically downgraded to more of an acquaintance. Dr. Riddell wanted to know the specifics of the story Robinson heard. His first defense was that no force had been used, and it was probably just the oppressive heat. Beyond that, Riddell told his friend, "He had complimented her too strongly, and gave as the reason for passing the compliment that it was the 'rutting season' for all animals." The doctor offered to meet with either of the Atkinsons and explain his behavior, presumably in a less graphic manner.

Thomas Atkinson was not mollified. He asked Robinson to tell Riddell to move out of town. For his part, Riddell said he was not moving from his home of over a decade, but he did proceed to get drunk.[63]

At about 6:30 a.m. on Friday morning, four days after the offending office exam, Constable Henry Ferguson, on his way to work, had walked only three blocks from his house when he heard shots fired. Hurrying to where a crowd stood gathered near the store and icehouse at Main Street and Prairie Avenue, a man walked to the officer and surrendered. It was Thomas Atkinson, covered in blood—both Riddell's and his own. He handed Ferguson two pistols and a Bowie knife. It was two days after the Atkinsons' first wedding anniversary.

Minutes earlier, Atkinson had followed Dr. Riddell to the store, where he saw the doctor enter carrying a basket and asking for Mr. White. That was as far as the doctor's business went. Atkinson ran through the store and chased Riddell into the backyard. A struggle ensued. Atkinson shot his pistols at Riddell, inflicting only one nonlethal wound under the doctor's right shoulder. He then pulled out his foot-long knife and plunged it twice into the doctor's back, piercing the aorta and adding another stab wound to the side that punctured the physician's left lung. Any of the three could have been the blow that killed him.

Even as his friend Robinson distanced himself from Dr. Riddell at the hearing, Houston's fellow physicians issued a strong statement of support. Eleven esteemed medical colleagues met at the office of Dr. G.M. Devereux and adopted resolutions to vindicate their slain friend. These doctors, under the heading "Medical Faculty of Houston," stated that as a scientist, Riddell had few peers in America. Moreover, they vehemently resolved that he was "incapable of anything derogatory to personal or professional honor" and that they and society must see "that no taint should attach to his well-earned good name."[64]

In the end, acting in defense of his wife's honor was good enough for the Houston justice system. Atkinson was turned loose. A postscript tells of what other observers thought of the Bayou City, however. After a "shooting scrape" on Preston Avenue in November 1875, the *Galveston Daily News* saw fit to publish a list of "crimes of this character" that occurred in Houston in the previous four years under a column subtitled "One of Many." It listed twenty-six murders, including that of Dr. Riddell. One sentence in the story stands out: "Only in one or two instances of the killings above mentioned were the perpetrators punished even by short terms in the Penitentiary, while a wretch, who killed a cow in Third Ward, was given a good term at Huntsville."[65]

A Murderous Scion

Before Benjamin Franklin Terry rode east to fame and death at the outset of the Civil War, he was in the sugar business in Fort Bend County with William Jefferson Kyle. Using slave labor, the two also built the first railroad in Texas. The partnership was so successful and lucrative that Terry named his youngest son Jefferson Kyle Terry.

Like his father, Kyle Terry was a large and imposing man. For his father, that size became the catalyst to leadership in the community and the Confederate army. For Kyle, it seems to have made him a bully. By the end of 1886, it could be noted that father and son also shared a dubious accomplishment. They had both legally gotten away with murder in Houston.

There the stories diverged. Frank Terry was only nineteen when he and his two youngest uncles were involved in a shooting melee at the horse races.

Kyle Terry, son of a Texas legend and frequent party to violent confrontations. *From the Fort Bend Museum.*

One turf man died, and the local newspapers kept the story quiet, presumably to preserve the honor of the alleged gentlemen involved. For Kyle Terry, the murder occurred when he was thirty-one years old, and the story got considerable notice—even a mention from the vaunted *New York Times.*[66]

The trouble started in a Main Street bar on a Saturday night. Kyle Terry was drinking in Charles Thavonat's saloon between Preston and Prairie, and he was armed. The beat cop, Henry Williams, was either in the bar or standing just outside when he tried to arrest Terry for the crime of carrying a pistol, but instead, Terry pulled the weapon and pointed it at the unarmed officer. Williams left to find reinforcements. Once banded, they found Terry down the street in another saloon. Again the pistol was brandished at the policemen, along with a string of "opprobrious epithets" such as "cow thief" and "son of a bitch," aimed specifically at Williams. Eventually, Terry was talked into surrendering and taken to the city jail. He bonded out, returning Monday morning to make a request that all charges be dropped.[67]

Leaving the calaboose about quarter of nine, Terry, arm in arm with his friend Sam Perkins, walked onto the sidewalk in front of the Market House on Travis. There he spotted Williams coming from the other direction, bound for the station house. He hurried ahead of Perkins, shouting at Officer Williams.

"You're the son of a bitch looking to kill me!" Terry yelled, even as he struggled to pull out his revolver, which was hung up on his waistband. By the time the gun was free, he was within six feet of Williams. He fired as Officer Williams stumbled backward. Citizens on the crowded Market Square began to scatter.

The Houston police station in which Kyle Terry was held. *From the Houston Police Department.*

Falling, the policeman grabbed Sam Johnson, an unfortunate black man who happened to be walking next to him. The two men fell off the sidewalk into the gutter of Preston Avenue. Johnson tried to move away as Terry stepped around him and fired three shots into Officer Williams, who was lying on his back.

The first bullet entered near the center of his chest, piercing the aorta and left ventricle of Williams' heart. It was enough to kill him, but Terry fired twice more, once into the groin and once into the thigh of the prostrate officer. Henry Williams, father of three, lay dead in the gutter, never given time to pull his own weapon.[68]

Some of Kyle Terry's friends rallied to his defense. Claims quickly surfaced that Officer Williams borrowed a shotgun late Saturday night with the idea to extract revenge for his abuse at the hands of Terry. That was the reason behind the shout on the street that Monday morning.

The dozen witnesses' statements that ran in the newspaper on Tuesday are a study in contradiction. The two spoke to each other, or Williams said nothing. There were four shots fired or only three. Williams was "trying to get his pistol out of his pocket," or he "did not have a pistol and I saw his hand."[69]

Terry was taken back to jail, but within two days, his case slipped from the Houston papers. Focus shifted to a notable murder from the previous year that had finally come to trial. Mrs. Phelps, a white resident who may have been operating a "disorderly house" in Fourth Ward, had shot and killed the estranged husband of her black next-door neighbor across their common yard after he loudly called her an "adulteress." She was acquitted by the all-white jury, whose members were asked to imagine their own wives or mothers so insolently abused.[70]

Meanwhile, Terry sat in jail, but not for long. His bail, initially denied by Judge Cox, a friend of Terry's late father, was set at $5,000 by the court of appeals. On March 6, Kyle Terry walked out of Harris County Jail. The case finally came to trial in December 1886, and to the surprise of some cynics, who assumed the fix was in, he was found guilty of second-degree murder. The sentence was two years, and he walked free upon the filing of an appeal.[71]

Kyle Terry returned to his Fort Bend County home and was soon elected county tax assessor. The political faction that backed Terry to victory was known as the Woodpeckers, made up of a small number of white Democrats and the mostly Republican black voters who, prior to 1868, had been completely disenfranchised. Fort Bend was one of a handful of Texas counties in which black slaves had outnumbered whites. Upon gaining the vote there, they also found new power.

Opposing Terry and the Woodpeckers were the Jaybirds, said to represent 90 percent of whites in the county, albeit those whites who were out of power as long as local African Americans could vote. The conservative Jaybirds were the faction supported by the former plantation-owning class, and that certainly included the Terrys. To the White Man's Union Jaybirds, Kyle Terry, son of one of Texas' greatest Confederate heroes, was considered "the worst Judas scalawag of them all."[72]

The election of 1888 proved to be the tipping point for general violence. Two Jaybird leaders were shot, one fatally. They responded by giving several leading Fort Bend blacks, elected officials, a restaurant owner, a barber and two schoolteachers ten hours to leave the county under threats of death. Most complied.

Terry turned up the heat when he condescendingly referred to his Jaybird opponent for office, Ned Gibson, as a "paper-collared dude" to close out a political rally. It touched off a heated feud between Terry and the entire Gibson clan. On election day, turnout was heavier than ever before, and the Woodpecker coalition won again. For white supremacist

Jaybirds, that was unacceptable. Making matters even more intolerable was the permanent smirk and open disdain shown by some of the Woodpeckers—Terry high among them, whether he was drunk or sober.[73]

The Woodpeckers planned an elegant celebration party and even invited some of their opponents. Several of the written invitations to the Jaybirds that did not get summarily trashed were readdressed to some of the black prostitutes who lived north of the tracks in Richmond. This was the catalyst for the next brush between Kyle Terry and the Gibsons in which he beat up Ned's brother Volney Gibson at the train depot. In retaliation, three Gibson brothers ambushed Terry at a Richmond boot shop. Unfortunately for them, their shots missed.

Blood was again drawn the following June when Kyle Terry, while drinking in a Wharton saloon, spotted Ned Gibson walking down the street. He stepped from the bar and unloaded a double-barrel shotgun into the man. As he was arrested for the murder, Terry took the time to wipe down his shotgun with a silk handkerchief before surrendering it to the Wharton sheriff.[74]

Terry missed the August 1889 street battle that was the culmination of the Jaybird-Woodpecker trouble. He had moved to Galveston, but Volney Gibson was right in the thick of it. It was a decided victory for the all-white faction, and many of their opponents left Fort Bend County altogether. The triumphant White Man's Union Jaybirds would control Fort Bend politics for seventy more years, but there was one score left to settle.[75]

Kyle Terry's trial for the murder of Ned Gibson was moved to Galveston, where it was believed an unbiased jury pool existed. On the morning

Ned Gibson was killed by Kyle Terry's shotgun blast in June 1889. *From the Fort Bend Museum.*

of January 21, 1890, at a preliminary hearing, Volney Gibson and six other Jaybirds stepped from an office as Terry started up the stairs to the courtroom. Without comment, they shot Terry seven times, including one bullet straight through the heart.[76]

And so Kyle Terry pulled off the very neat trick of being murdered while in the courthouse for his own murder trial. He is buried in Houston at Glenwood Cemetery next to his parents and not too terribly far from one of his victims: Houston police officer Henry Williams.

JUDGE LYNCH

The mostly African American community of Sunny Side sits in Waller County, a short distance north of Brookshire. It was named after a plantation owned by Philip Cuney, and after the Civil War, many of the families of the freed slaves remained in the neighborhood. Though slavery was over, life for the former Texas bondsmen was by no means easy in the 1880s and '90s. Sharecropping often left rural blacks just marginally better off than they were before emancipation. Crime in African American communities was often seen to be a larger problem than elsewhere in the southern countryside, and those who entered the state's prison system found themselves hired out—right back in the fields working for free. In rural Texas, as it was elsewhere in the South, it was easy to find poverty and all that went with it.

Late on the night of Thursday, April 29, 1897, reports of a triple murder came into the county seat of Hempstead. Henry Daniels and two young girls were murdered twenty-four hours prior, and the "hut" that they occupied was set afire. Authorities quickly made the fifteen-mile trip to the scene.[77]

What they found was shockingly brutal. Daniels, described as "an old negro," had been stabbed to death trying to protect his teenaged stepdaughter, Maria, and an unnamed seven-year-old girl. The two young girls were "ravished" and then killed. The bodies of Daniels and Maria were placed in their tiny home, which was then set on fire. The younger girl, her skull smashed, was thrown down the well. Stories of this outrage reached Houston on the lips of train passengers even before local newspapers could set the tale into type.[78]

The story, however, was only beginning. Folks living in the Sunny Side community already knew that Henry Daniels was no paragon of virtue. For one thing, he was somehow involved with the robbery of a Brenham man the previous fall. Allegedly, the theft was pulled off by the Thomas boys, who were long considered a neighborhood menace to "life and property." The perpetrators got away with sixty-five dollars, thirty of which was given to Daniels. Whether he had an active part in the heist or was simply holding the money was uncertain.[79]

What was abundantly clear, however, was that twenty-year-old Louis Thomas and his three teenaged brothers, Benny, Jim and Aaron, decided on that Wednesday night in late April that Daniels had held his half of the loot long enough. They headed to his place with the conviction to either get it back or kill him. Upon finding out that the money had already been spent, they made good on the latter proposition. When they were done, they set the fire to cover their tracks.[80]

The initial reaction to the house fire in Sunny Side was muted, but when the inhabitants couldn't be found, the ruins were searched and the grisly discovery made. Bloodhounds from the nearby Steele Plantation were summoned, and the dogs led the searchers directly to the Thomas place. The Thomas boys had been living alone, and their neighbors considered them "the worst set in this country." Their father, Richmond Thomas, lived within sight of the Daniels home. When authorities searched Richmond's premises, they found another bloody shirt belonging to one of the boys.

The questioning didn't take long to produce results. The brothers, some still wearing bloody clothing, confessed to everything and named three other accomplices: Fayette Rhoan, in his early twenties; Willie Williams, possibly a cousin to the Thomas brothers; and thirty-five-year-old Will Gates, a newcomer to the Sunny Side community. One by one they were rounded up and assembled in a house to await their fate.

The reported story was that just before midnight on Friday the thirtieth, a mob appeared outside the house, overpowered those who held the seven prisoners and hauled them out into the woods "toward the Brazos Bottom." The group of vigilantes was mixed race, but African Americans from Sunny Side predominated. Almost immediately, gunfire was heard. By the first glimmer of light Saturday morning, the "stark" and "lifeless" bodies of six of the seven young men were all hanging from a lone oak tree that stood near the road. The *Houston Post* reporter called it a "fearful sight and one that would appall the stoutest." Willie Williams was unaccounted for.[81]

As Saturday wore on, some in Waller County began to reconsider at least two of the lynchings. Even as newspapers reported that "the white residents of Hempstead…are upholding the negroes who did the hanging," others in the county were questioning whether Rhoan and

The *Houston Post* artist's eyewitness depiction of the Sunny Side Lynching, 1897. *From the Harris County Archives.*

Gates were actually involved in the murders at the Daniels place. Waller County sheriff Lipscomb stated that he thought two of the hanged men might have been innocent.

The Thomas brothers and Gates were cut down and buried in a mass grave near the base of the tree on which they met their end. Fayette Rhoan's body was claimed by "his people who will give him decent burial."[82]

Even in a state where total racial equality was never seriously considered, six bodies hanging from one tree still had to be explained. Saturday's newspapers from Norfolk to Sacramento ran stories of the lynching on their front pages. Sheriff Lipscomb, who had not initially traveled to the scene of the violence, was called to Austin to meet with Governor Culberson. His reason for inaction: he was guarding his jail to prevent an expected mob from lynching three other black citizens, who were being held for the murder of an older black woman. He did make clear that Willie Williams was now in his custody.[83]

Governor Culberson offered a reward for members of the mob, and Sheriff Lipscomb announced that he "had strong evidence as to the identity of about a dozen of those who took part." The press was skeptical. The *Post* opined that it would be next to impossible to single out the country folk guilty of the executions, "thus the whole affair will be relegated to the past, another chapter in the history of 'Judge Lynch,' who knows of no appeal, technicalities or reversals."[84]

They were right. Lipscomb went so far as to suggest that "white men did the work and that the alleged confession of the Thomas boys was a myth." But that was the last of the bluster. A day later, the sheriff backtracked about knowing the identity of mob members and said he only knew Williams to be safe, not that he had him in custody. He even went so far as to claim that he had no idea he had been talking to a reporter.[85]

One week after the hangings, a report surfaced that Fayette Rhoan was wanted for the rape of a twelve-year-old girl in Luling and was therefore not innocent at all. Even before that, talk of bringing the lynchers to justice vanished from local newspapers. On May 11, less than two weeks after the rampage at Henry Daniels' place, a new outrage hit the state's papers. Three black men in Rosebud were arrested for breaking into a house with the intent to rape a seventeen-year-old white girl. After being held in the Rosebud jail for the better part of the week, a mob, none of whom could be recognized, took the three from custody and hanged them all from a small tree. The sheriff in Falls County solemnly told the press that he was "going to do all in (his) power to bring the proper parties to justice."[86]

AVENGING ANGEL

Glenwood Cemetery, the final resting place for Howard Hughes and many other exemplars of Houston's high and mighty, is full of marble angels. Most wear melancholy countenances or tender half-smiles, all except for the angel standing guard over the grave of William Dunovant.

A South Carolina–bred rice and sugar planter and would-be railroad magnate, Dunovant and business partner William T. Eldridge founded the Cane Belt Railroad in 1898. As the name suggests, at first, the Cane Belt transported sugar cane from Dunovant's plantation near the town of Bonus ten miles north to Lakeside, near Eagle Lake, but eventually the line was extended from Sealy all the way to the Gulf.[87]

Perhaps that was an overambitious plan, because by 1902, the Cane Belt was floundering. Dunovant's shares were bought out, and he was

The "Avenging Angel" at William Dunovant's grave. *From the Mike Vance collection.*

removed from his position as president. Eldridge, also a sugar planter, stayed on the board as vice-president. Dunovant was none too pleased with that arrangement.

Yes, the Cane Belt's cargoes may have been sweet, but by August of 1902, things were definitely sour between Dunovant and Eldridge. Dunovant reportedly went around Eagle Lake calling Eldridge a liar, a cheat and "a dog-faced sonofabitch" and publicly threatened to kill him.

Dunovant never got the chance to make good on that promise. On August 11, as Dunovant boarded a passenger car of a train Eldridge was already aboard, Eldridge got the drop on him. After emptying his revolver into Dunovant, Eldridge pounced upon his bleeding body and pistol-whipped Dunovant's head hard enough to lacerate the scalp.

Dunovant's corpse was taken to Glenwood for burial. The "Avenging Angel," brandishing its fierce sword and with crazy eyes that look like a mix between Mike Singletary and the Children of the Corn, was commissioned by Dunovant's sister. It truly lives up to its billing as "a specter bent on revenge."

It turns out that the Dunovant family would not content themselves with leaving their lust for payback in supernatural hands.

After Eldridge was charged with Dunovant's murder, he bonded out and returned to his home in Eagle Lake, a town full of Dunovant's friends, family members and supporters. Barely two months after Dunovant's demise, a partisan named W.T. Cobb blasted his shotgun at Eldridge as he ascended his front steps. Cobb missed and was charged with attempted murder. He was acquitted on September 26, 1903. Strike one for the "Avenging Angel."

The months dragged on. Eldridge's attorneys reset his case over and over again, and Eldridge defiantly remained in Eagle Lake.

Team "Avenging Angel" struck again on June 6, 1904. W.E. Calhoun, Dunovant's brother-in-law, sniped at Eldridge out of a second-story window in downtown Eagle Lake. Calhoun's

William T. Eldridge. *From the Fort Bend Museum.*

aim was true—the 30-30 Winchester shell ripped through Eldridge's right lung and chest just above the heart, continued through his left hand and finally lodged in the side of a windowsill at the Eagle Lake depot.

Calhoun was arrested as he attempted to leave the building from which the shot was fired, but none of the witnesses on the scene would testify against him. He was no-billed by a Colorado County grand jury, which was probably of lesser import to Calhoun than the fact that Eldridge had miraculously survived the attack. Strike two.

Eldridge finally *did* get the message that perhaps living in Eagle Lake was not exactly conducive to his continued existence on the planet, so on July Fourth, he announced his planned move to Houston, along with his resignation from the Cane Belt Railroad.

In November, Eldridge finally had his day in court and was acquitted on the grounds of self-defense. You'd think that would be the end of it, but by this time, Eldridge was out for blood. Weeks after Calhoun was no-billed, he had the rather déjà vu misfortune to board a train Eldridge was already riding, and Eldridge wasted no time in reprising the original murder by filling Dunovant's kinsman with lead before Calhoun could draw his pistol.

Calhoun's body was taken to Glenwood and interred next to Dunovant's ferocious-yet-hapless "Avenging Angel," who had now officially struck out.

As for Eldridge, after again pleading self-defense and again winning an acquittal, he wound up in Sugar Land, where in 1906, he allied himself with Galveston's Kempner family. The partnership bought twenty thousand acres of sugar plantation and refinery, most of which was owned and operated by Frank Terry and William Jefferson Kyle. No doubt Kyle Terry visited there as a child. The business later reorganized and modernized under the new owners as mighty Imperial Sugar, with Eldridge serving as manager. He also bought and sold seven railroads in his remaining years, which sounds as if Eldridge must have been quite comfortable, despite the two holes in his body from Calhoun's 30-30 shell.[88]

With a population of 200, Sugar Land was on the point of withering away when Eldridge arrived; by the time he died in 1932, it had 2,500 residents. Today, Imperial Sugar is the oldest business in Texas. That's one reason Eldridge Road and Eldridge Parkway both bear his name.

4

HEIGHTS HOUSE OF HORROR

Extra! Extra! Read all about it!
Five slaughtered in Houston Heights house of horror!

So the Houston newsboys on downtown street corners might have cried on the afternoon of March 16, 1910, for earlier that day, Harris County sheriff Archie Anderson walked in on one of the grisliest spectacles in area history.

Exactly when the brutal bludgeonings took place was unknown. The victims had been dead several days by the time they were discovered, and Anderson said that he had to air the house out for hours before he could even begin to investigate the crime scene. The carnage moved more than a few papers, and the *Houston Chronicle* was not above toasting its own success, noting that its extra edition smashed sales records.[89]

The city of Houston was already a little on edge. Only one day before the gruesome discovery in the Heights, Texas Company founder Joseph Cullinan was shot by a disgruntled employee on Texas Avenue in front of Christ Church Cathedral. Tank-gauging engineer H.W. Glass fired a single bullet into Cullinan's stomach as the two argued on the sidewalk during the middle of the lunch hour. As salacious as the shooting of a top city magnate was, the murder of an entire family quickly knocked it from the news.[90]

The sheriff and his deputies found five bodies stacked in a heap between two beds in an unpainted three-room cabin at 732 Ashland Street. They were the corpses of twenty-three-year-old Gus Schultz, a lineman for

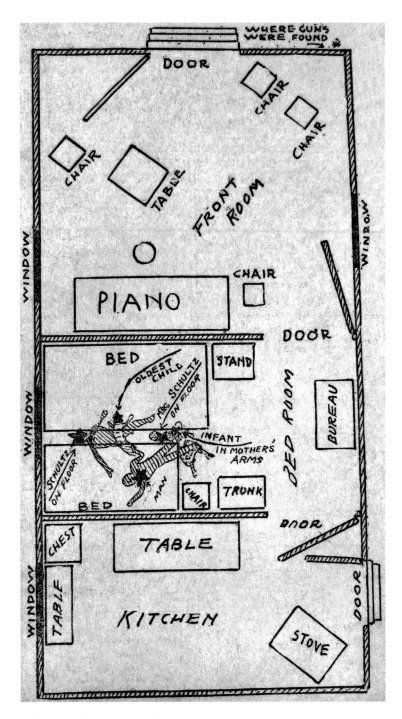

A diagram of bodies in the Heights murder house as it appeared in the
Houston Post. From the Harris County Archives.

HL&P; his young wife, Alice; their two children, ages three years and five months; and their lodger, Walter Eichmann, a painter. The infant was cradled in the arms of her dead mother. Bits of skull and shreds of clothing were scattered all about the eight- by twelve-foot bedroom, and the beds, floors, window shades and walls halfway to the ceiling were saturated with pooled and clotted blood. It appeared that at least some of the victims put up a struggle.[91]

The home sat in the southwest portion of the city of Houston Heights. It was not one of the three-story Victorian mansions that lined the Boulevard or even the comfortable bungalows that would appear a decade later. This portion of the Heights was predominantly home to working-class whites, some of whom were employed at nearby factories or railroad yards. It bordered a segregated black neighborhood that sat only a few streets to the west.[92]

At the small shack on Ashland, Sheriff Anderson searched for clues. There weren't many. Attention was first drawn to the grisly crime scene when Maggie Nelson, an African American woman who did the couple's laundry, noticed three guns lying under the building, just outside the home's front door. Nelson told the Schultzes' next-door neighbor, who in turn called the sheriff about the two rifles and the old, double-barrel shotgun. The score of clothing items that Nelson had hung on the clothesline the previous Friday still flapped in the breeze.[93]

Both doors to the cottage were locked up tight from the inside. Curtains and shades were carefully drawn. Sheriff Anderson forced a window to gain entry. Once the lawmen got past the awful stench and into the bedroom, they determined that the first to fall was the husband, Gus Schultz, known to his family as Tab. His mauled body was at the bottom of the beastly pile, obscured by the forms of his wife and children, who were dressed for bed. Eichmann, still clad in trousers and an undershirt, lay on top. All five faces and heads were smashed in from the front.[94]

Neighbors, who flocked to the murder house in droves, told police that Gus and Alice Schultz, a happy couple with a harmonious marriage, hosted a beery little living room shindig on Friday night, March 10. They danced, and people played guitar and piano. Several guests filtered in and out of the party that night, but none reported any incident. When the soiree broke up, Gus Schultz walked to the nearby grocery and saloon. He enjoyed a glass of beer with friends and then headed back home.

In fact, though the sheriff's team searched until the wee hours, the officers could initially find no motive whatsoever for "the bloody carnival." The best

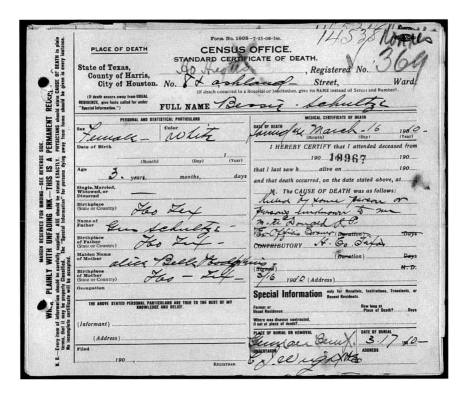

Bessie Schultz's death certificate. *From the Texas Department of State Health Services.*

they could surmise, it was the work of a "fiend who may have developed a homicidal mania and satisfied his lust for blood" at the expense of the Schultzes. Nor could the investigators locate a murder weapon. One by one, chairs, tools and other heavy objects were examined and eliminated. Outbuildings were searched. Mrs. Jenkins, the woman who had called the sheriff, preliminarily identified the victims, by then stretched side by side in the front parlor. Schultz's brother-in-law and Eichmann's ex-wife arrived to confirm the identifications.[95]

The Schultz family, of which Gus was the seventh son and one of eleven children, took charge of the decomposing bodies. Rites for the slain Schultzes took place at the C.J. Wright Funeral Parlor on Travis, and the father and his children were buried in the family plot at the German Cemetery less than twenty-four hours after they were found. The Hodgkinses, parents of Mrs. Schultz, held an earlier ceremony and privately interred their daughter at Hollywood Cemetery. Though they lived in nearby Brunner, Mr. and Mrs. Hodgkins had never seen their youngest granddaughter.[96]

By the afternoon following the funerals, the sheriff's attention focused on one of the previous week's party guests. Alexander Horton "Sandy" Sheffield, a "big-boned oiler" at the Houston Ice and Brewing Company, had once been "familiarly friendly" with Alice Schultz. In fact, the tall, athletic Sheffield often stayed at the Schultz home until Eichmann began lodging there.[97]

The rumor mill was hot with alleged ties between Alice and another man, presumed by most to be Sheffield. Houston newspaper reporters followed their own leads, learning from Goggan's music store that while Gus Schultz had made the first payment on the piano his wife wanted, the second payment was placed by "another man." A jewelry store employee told the *Post* that Mrs. Schultz had freely admitted that this "other man" was the "the only man that she loved and would ever love." Much was read into Sheffield's return to the "charnel house" on the Sunday before the bodies were found. When asked the whereabouts of the Schultzes, Sheffield told Mrs. Jenkins, the neighbor, that perhaps the whole family had "gone fishing and had been drowned."[98]

Other rumors surfaced. One story held that a "strange Mexican" was seen leaving the area and later took a blood-soaked suit to a cleaner. Yet Anderson's prime suspect was Sheffield, the grandson and namesake of Sam Houston's aide-de-camp, Alexander Horton. Anderson scoffed at the Mexican theory. No criminal would be so stupid as to take a bloody suit to a cleaners after wearing it while killing five people nearby, he said. Sheriff Archie Anderson arrested Sandy Sheffield at the brewery on the afternoon of March 17 and promised reporters that he would explain why later. Sheffield told police that his arrest was not unexpected.[99]

Problems plagued the case against Sheffield from the start. The *Post* headline even stated, "No Direct Evidence Against the Prisoner." It was all circumstantial. In Anderson's eyes, however, Sheffield had a clear motive. Though Sheffield was married, Anderson believed he still held a candle for Alice Schultz. As the *Chronicle* grandiloquently expounded on this theory, the slaughter was believed to have been committed "in a fit of jealous rage by someone who had been friendly with Mrs. Schultz and who, unhappy because she belonged to another, succumbed to a paroxysm of feeling and slaughtered her and all about her."[100]

The weekend after the Wednesday discovery of the battered bodies passed, and headlines could only lament, "Murder Mystery Deepens." It had been days since the story broke, and authorities still had no solid clues. The house of horrors was a magnet for thousands of curious onlookers, who

Sheriff Archie Anderson poses in front of the county jail. *From the Harris County Sheriff's Office.*

stomped all over the grounds and wandered into the unlocked home itself to inspect the "little death chamber." Others in Houston Heights carefully avoided passing near it. On Friday afternoon, workers hired by Gus Schultz's family sorted out every piece of furniture from the little cottage that bore any evidence of the carnage and burned them in the yard.[101]

Forensics was a fledgling science in 1910, and contamination of a crime scene was an unknown idea. Though the concept of unique fingerprints was known and had even figured in Mark Twain's *Life on the Mississippi,* it wasn't until the St. Louis World's Fair of 1904 and an appearance by a Scotland Yard sergeant that the idea began to creep into American police departments. Harris County sheriff's deputies had found what may have been a bloody thumb mark on the sill of the window where the killer made his escape from the Schultz house, but it received no further mention in the press.[102]

The lawmen did suspect that multiple weapons had been used, something blunt and something sharp, but no such items presented themselves. They also surmised that Eichmann was sick and sleeping in the children's bed instead of on his customary kitchen floor pallet. He remained in the back of the house during the Friday party. This would have allowed the perpetrator to get the jump on him. A news leak told of a cloth found over Eichmann's face, possibly meaning chloroform was used.

Investigators searched the railroad tracks that passed only fifty feet from the murder scene under the presumption that the killer fled that way under cover of night. They found nothing. The guns tossed under the house were definitively said to have belonged to the Schultzes and Eichmann, including a newly discovered .38 pistol that had been on a shelf in the hen house, an outbuilding that had already been searched. Removal of the firearms led police to believe that the murderer had known the victims fairly well since visitors to the house were used to seeing them leaning against a wall.

Finally, a week after the bodies were found, two railroad detectives searching on their own pulled the supposed murder weapon from the well behind the house with a grappling hook. It was a hatchet with a sharp blade on one side of the head and a crushing mallet on the other. Brown stains on the handle were thought to be blood, even though the tool had been sitting in several feet of water. Like the hen house, the well had been searched a week earlier.

Meanwhile, Sandy Sheffield sat quietly in a cell, visited by his brother, his father, his lawyers and once by his loyal wife and crying children. For a week, he roosted in the red-and-white brick Victorian jail on Capitol Avenue at the bayou, not even getting a hearing before a judge. He gave his first statement seven days after his arrest, still vehemently proclaiming his innocence and saying that his patience was worn thin; enough time had elapsed for the county to prove its case. The next day, he made bail, and after signatories put up $1,000, Sheffield went home to his family.

Looking "tall and clean," he spoke to reporters from his front porch on 16th near Railroad Street while he held his squirmy and affectionate daughter, Mildred, in his arms. His side of the story sounded perfectly plausible, but it must have been particularly galling to those authorities convinced that he was the dastardly murderer. Sheffield said that he and his friend Frank Turney left the party before 9:00 p.m. that Friday, and a handful of guests were still there dancing in the Schultzes' parlor. As for his Sunday visit, he happened past the home and saw that two cows had wandered through the open gate and were threatening to sully the hanging laundry. He chased them out and then told Mrs. Jenkins to alert Mrs. Schultz to his help. It all fit tidily.[103]

The story was so solid that it brought a stall in the case for over a year. The grand jury refused to indict. Crowds eventually stopped gathering on Ashland Street. Sheriff Archie Anderson ran for reelection and won. Sandy Sheffield went to work each day in the engine room at the brewery and went back to his family every evening. Neighbors described the Sheffields as a happy couple, but some added that the wife was pathetically clingy. The quest for a conviction in the Schultz case seemingly sat on a back burner. That is, until June 1911, when Frank Turney, the carpenter friend of Sandy Sheffield who was misidentified by the papers as "Turner" one year prior, coughed up a lurid confession.[104]

Why it took fifteen months to feel this prick on his conscience was not clear, nor was Turney's reason for accompanying his friend that night in March 1910, when he was certain that Sheffield did "something awful in the house." Turney also offered no description of how Sheffield allegedly looked when he emerged from the home.

The confession sequence allegedly began when Turney shared a portion of his story with a relative, a person who in turn alerted two Houston policemen to an impending meeting between Turney and Sheffield. Detectives Dave Robinson and Charles Cain wasted no time in heading for Houston Heights, even though the town was outside their jurisdiction. Arriving at the appointed spot, the two gumshoes slipped into a roadside gully on their bellies. There they lay for almost an hour while the conversation between the two suspects took place.

"Only you and the woman know anything about the case," the officers heard Sheffield tell Turney. "She is where she can't talk, and if it ever comes out, it will come from you."[105]

The detectives reported this hot lead to HPD chief "Duff" Voss, who in turn relayed it to Sheriff Anderson. Within hours, Voss and Anderson were personally grilling young Frank Turney. The duo told reporters that the new confession "coupled exactly with other facts in possession of the officers." Even without the confession, the authorities claimed confidence in the evidence they had gathered.

It certainly unleashed a flurry of new details to the public. In spite of being married, witnesses suggested that Sandy Sheffield spent most of his waking, nonworking hours in the company of Alice Schultz until her husband, Gus, had tried to put a halt to it. It was so noticeable that a previous Schultz landlady had asked them to move from her respectable boardinghouse. Sheffield and a seventeen-year-old female had spent most of the afternoon prior to the infamous Friday night party at the little house on Ashland with Alice Schultz and Walter Eichmann, who had stayed home sick from work.

It was when Eichmann moved in with the Schultzes that Sheffield's jealousy grew. He was certain that he had been supplanted, the sheriff surmised. On that Friday afternoon, as the two women giggled, Alice Schultz, looking "awful cute" in a low-cut, pale pink dress "cut high above the shoe tops and close fitting all around," slipped into the kitchen, where Eichmann was resting on his pallet. Through the half-opened door, Sheffield saw her hug and kiss the new boarder. According to the police, that sent the spurned lover over the edge.

Turney said that late that night, Sheffield enlisted him and another friend, Lydia Howell, to stand watch at the front and back gates to the Schultzes' yard while he used a pass key to slip inside. The horrific descriptions of five murders committed with such rage later drove Lydia Howell insane, forcing her commitment to a state asylum, but not before she had also accused Sheffield of the savage deed in an interview with Sherriff Anderson.[106]

Another entirely new twist came when the sheriff announced that the five bodies had been dragged into the ghastly pile as late as two days after the killings. Following these bombshells in the *Post* was a most prescient paragraph: "This, however, is all conjecture. For that matter, the whole thing has been conjecture, save the physical facts that the family and the boarder were killed in a brutal manner."[107]

Once again, Sandy Sheffield sat in Harris County Jail, charged with the murder of Alice Schultz and the four others, saying little except to his lawyers. Turney initially faced five murder indictments as well, but they became charges of accessory before the fact. He did not have the wherewithal to bond out, but Sheffield was back home by October, thanks to a cadre of friends and family in East Texas.[108]

When his case reached court in December 1911, three witnesses and the lead defense counsel, toiling in another courtroom, were not present at the docket call. Rather than agree to the defense's request for a two-day postponement, Judge Robinson continued the case until April. When that date arrived, it was the state's turn to ask for a continuance. The prosecution was missing a key witness, Sallie McClure, a black woman who overheard Sheffield make threats against the Schultz family. She testified before the grand jury back in July, but her absence at trial posed a problem for the state. Another continuance was granted. Just as in December, the prosecution ordered that its star witness, Frank Turney, remain in his cell.[109]

Turney's confinement would end sooner than expected, though. On October 11, 1912, Harris County district attorney Richard Maury dropped all five counts against Turney, allowing him to walk from the jail a free man. Maury stated that aside from the limited comments in his confession about standing at the gate, there was nothing else to connect Turney to the crimes. More to the point, perhaps, was the second part of the statement admitting that Turney's confession "was obtained under circumstances and conditions that would not justify its admission as evidence against him." Among other problems, there had been a "partial promise" of immunity.[110]

For any careful observer, it was handwriting on the wall. On May 14, 1913, the *Galveston Daily News* ran a tiny piece announcing the dismissal of all charges against A.H. Sheffield at the insistence of D.A. Maury, who stated that "he had not sufficient evidence upon which to base hopes of

conviction." Coverage in Houston was equally scant. After the media storm that followed the case for so long, it was a whimpering end.[111]

It appears that after living under the worst type of cloud for over three years, Sandy Sheffield reentered the realm of the work-a-day life. His son, Alexander Horton Sheffield Jr., was born in 1916, and the census of 1920 shows the then-forty-one-year-old Sheffield employed in the ice plant, which was no longer making beer during Prohibition, and living with his wife, Katherine, and their three children. He chose to remain in the Houston area for the remainder of his days, retiring from the ice business and dying a widower in Channelview on August 17, 1968.[112]

Lydia Howell, only eighteen at the time she allegedly stood lookout and possibly the young woman who had been present in the Schultz home on the afternoon of March 10, had been sent to the Southwestern Insane Asylum on the south side of San Antonio. By 1913, she was back in Houston Heights with her family and would remain there for at least three years. After that, she slipped from view.[113]

Evidence indicates that Frank Turney quickly recovered from the poor health that was cited as an additional reason for his release from jail in 1912. He married a young woman named Lydia Lee, and the two had several children. Following his release, he continued working in northwest Houston as a carpenter and contractor, going by his full name of Thomas Franklin Turney. Tragedy was not finished with him, however.[114]

By March 1941, the Turney children had a long-running feud with the seven Biggs children who lived down the street. Their father, by most accounts a bitter man, may well have set the tone for the family. One altercation between the kids was over a yo-yo. On March 29, it was about a rubber ball. That fight escalated to rock throwing and ended in a gun battle between pistol-toting, sixteen-year-old Marvin Biggs and fifty-two-

The Southwestern Insane Asylum in San Antonio where Lydia Howell was sent. *From the Mike Vance collection.*

61

year-old Frank Turney, who fired a shotgun at least once "to scare the Biggs children." One of the several shots fired pierced the heart of Mildred Biggs, age seven, killing her. Police swiftly determined that the bullet came from her own brother's handgun, but someone figured he had suffered enough for his deed. He was not charged. For his role, Turney was charged with assault with intent to murder, once again on the edges of tragedy. Frank Turney died at home in Houston in 1950.[115]

5
THE ROARING TWENTIES FADE

THE KILLING OF BABIES

There is no house at 1805 Pierce Street ninety-two years later. There are virtually no houses for blocks around the address that sits in the shadow of the Pierce Elevated, but in 1922, it was a quiet residential neighborhood anchored by the Sacred Heart Catholic Church and School a few blocks west. St. Joseph's Hospital, which would consume much of the area, was a growing facility of over three hundred beds, confined to the corner of Pierce and Crawford.

On the night of Wednesday, April 19, Horace J. Mathis, who had been renting the place at 1805 Pierce for a few years, called his three young children back from the Williamses' home next door where they'd been playing. He tucked them all into bed just before ten o'clock and then headed off to his night shift at the power plant for the Houston Electric Company. His father, Yulee Mathis, lived in the same house and would watch the kids, as he had for the last month. The oldest of the three was looking forward to his ninth birthday when he awoke, and the two Mathis men no doubt had something planned. Since Horace's wife, Jean, had abruptly run off a week before, things had been difficult for the family, but not impossible.[116]

Before six o'clock the next morning, William Yulee, age nine; Elizabeth, age eight; and Horace Louise, age six, were all dead. Their grandfather had alerted the police that he found the bodies when he climbed out of bed around 5:40 a.m., over half an hour later than his normal wake-up time. The elder Mathis stated that he found the four gas jets on the kitchen stove going full blast. Though his room adjoined that of the children, and he swore the door between them was ajar, Yulee Mathis reported noticing no smell of gas until he rose from his bed. Then again, the windows in the grandfather's room were open, while those where the children slept, all tucked into one bed, were shut tight.[117]

Not only were the windows closed, but someone had also stuffed crumpled newspapers into the spaces under the doors and into each wide crack in the floorboards and walls in that part of the frame house. An investigator later testified that a piece of magazine was even stuffed into the keyhole on Grandpa Mathis' door.

The door from the kitchen to the children's room stood completely open. According to Dr. James Bost, who had come to the scene from nearby St. Joseph's, the spreading gas killed the three grade-schoolers in less than an hour. The white coverlet on their bed showed a spot of blood, presumed by authorities to be stained when one child was sickened by the asphyxiation.[118]

Horace Mathis, barely able to speak to reporters when he returned from work, said that the three children were due to go with their grandfather on Saturday to "be placed in the Baptist Academy at San Marcos." The school was not cheap. Tuition was $500 for each child, and no discounts were given for students who joined a term already in progress.[119]

Jean Mathis got word at her new boardinghouse at Port Arthur that her children were all dead. She headed for Houston that night but missed a connecting train at Beaumont. She didn't arrive until the twenty-first.

The funeral took place on Friday afternoon, and scores of the Mathis children's classmates attended. The three youngsters were buried at Forest Park Cemetery.[120]

Harris County district attorney E.T. Branch conducted the investigation personally, and it quickly centered on the one man who was known to have been with the children at the time of their deaths—their grandfather and namesake of the dead boy, Yulee S. Mathis. He was arrested the same day his grandchildren were interred.

From the start, Mathis protested his innocence. His counsel from the firm of Johnson and Gilmore filed numerous motions, but they struggled to get Mathis sprung from jail.

In September, exactly five months after the triple murders, Yulee Mathis came to trial. Again, his lawyers were ready with a flurry of motions for Judge C.W. Robinson. There were objections to the small jury pool and a request for a continuance since one of the key defense witnesses had moved

The Harris County Jail around 1925. This building contained a gallows for executions, which were carried out by individual counties at the time. *From the San Jacinto Museum of History.*

to Fort Worth. With a statement that the court planned to start another murder trial the following day, all the motions were denied.[121]

The big courtroom filled with spectators, some of whose rowdiness brought a rebuke from the judge. All the seats on the main floor and in the balcony were filled, and "standing room was at a premium," even in the corridor outside. Deputies ejected more than twenty people, and Judge Robinson warned, "If they won't get seated, bring them up here and I'll sit them down so hard they won't get up for awhile."

Investigators and experts led off the parade of witnesses at 9:00 a.m. Detective George Andrews told of finding a rusty railroad spike, likely taken from a pile nearby, that might have been used to pry open the kitchen door. A hole cut in the screen door was also mentioned. The men were followed by Lizzie Williams, who lived next door to the Mathis house. She recounted Yulee Mathis calling through her door to say he had discovered the children's bodies. They were still dressed in the clothes they had been wearing the night before when they played at her house.[122]

By mid-afternoon, it was the mother's turn. Jean Balcom had gotten a divorce and already remarried during the five-month interim. The slender, pretty twenty-nine-year-old woman was dressed "in deepest mourning," including a black veil that obscured her face. She had been beaten "incessantly" for the entirety of their marriage, Mrs. Balcom testified. The press did not report her motive for leaving her children with such a father.[123]

Defense attorneys had tried to present alternate theories for the killings—one accidental and two malicious. Among the names the defense put forth were Jean Mathis Balcom; neighbor Tobe Williams, who had been in the home the night of the killings; and Paul Balcom, the man Jean Mathis had run to in Port Arthur. The missing defense witness, Mrs. T.P. Walsh, was supposed to testify that she had seen a "high-powered automobile without lights" pull up near the Mathis house on the night of the killings.[124]

Throughout the long day, defendant Mathis betrayed no emotion as he sat next to his son-in-law, Wash Minksy, the son of Polish immigrants. A daughter and his son, Horace, also sat next to their father at various points during the trial, and on the final day, Yulee Mathis held another of his grandchildren on his lap.[125]

It was late in the day before Yulee Mathis took the stand in his own defense. Mathis was asked point blank if he had killed the children. "I did not," he replied.

There was a scandalous confession during his testimony to be sure. Yulee Mathis stoically admitted that he and his daughter-in-law, Jean, carried on a sexual relationship. She was the one who made the advances, the elder Mathis told the prosecutor. It had begun at the beginning of the year, not long after he had left his hometown of Hearne and moved in with his son Horace's family. It was the worst thing he had ever done, Mathis said, and he was "ashamed and sorry for it."[126]

With that revelation still buzzing around the packed courtroom, the children's cuckolded father, Horace, took the stand. It was after seven o'clock in the evening. He began with a recounting of events prior to his leaving for work on that fateful night. It had started with the two Mathis men walking to a nearby store to use the telephone. Horace had persuaded his father to turn down a job offer for carpentry work that would have taken the senior Mathis out of town. The son needed him at home. The call made, the two headed back to the house.

On the way, they met their neighbor Williams. He came to the Mathis house, where they discussed the runaway Mrs. Mathis. If Horace "would be good to his wife, Williams was sure she would come back by Saturday," one paper reported.[127]

Horace Mathis reiterated that the door connecting his father's room with the children's was ajar when he left but supposed that the wind might have blown it shut and locked the spring latch. He also confirmed that the transom over the outside door in Yulee Mathis' room had a half-broken glass. The defense counsel was pointing to that as the ventilation that saved the grandfather's life, given that the state argued no one could have lived an hour if the door to the children's room was ajar.

Finally, the state asked Horace to comment on his father's total lack of outward emotion during the trial. "He is not that kind of man," Mathis said, adding that he had never seen his father shed a tear in his life.

E.T. Branch made the final summation of the state's case personally. If Yulee Mathis was found guilty, Branch said, "I want him to receive the full punishment provided by the court's charge—death."[128]

The defense, led by Knox Gilmore, won two vital motions, and Judge Robinson charged the jurors that they could only consider the sexual relationship between Jean Mathis and her father-in-law as it pertained to the case at hand. The second special instruction was that if they believed "from the evidence that Tobe Williams, Paul Balcom, Jean Mathis or any person other than the defendant turned on the gas" or if they had a reasonable doubt, then they should vote not guilty. The judge even cautioned the jury about conviction in a case where all the evidence was circumstantial.[129]

The court's next pressing case notwithstanding, the twelve men on the jury deliberated for twenty hours. When they returned, the verdict was guilty. The sentence was only ten years, attributed to the circumstantial evidence and lack of motive, as well as to Mathis' age at sixty-two. The *Post* writer

The Yulee Mathis jury verdict in the handwriting of the foreman, J.H. Suttles. *From the Harris County District Clerk Archives.*

speculated that he might be the oldest person ever convicted of murder in Harris County.[130]

Yulee Mathis spoke to reporters after he had unflinchingly listened to his fate. Though he didn't say much about the impending term at the penitentiary, he did go on at length about his son's marital troubles.

Horace Mathis also spent time with the press. He admitted hoping for a hung jury and suggested that not enough time was spent on the investigation.

"I realize that my father could be guilty of killing my babies," he said. "But in his continued denials he seems to be telling the truth. I realize also that someone else could have killed the children for a purpose. As sure as you live, there is more to learn about the crime than what has been heard in the court room."[131]

AFTER THE CRASH

The story is that Houston fared pretty well during the Great Depression. It's true that thanks to Jesse Jones' strong-arming of his fellow financiers, not a single major bank in the city failed. But there was no shortage of foreclosures and shattered American dreams. Soup kitchens blossomed, and a major tent city sprawled beyond the tracks behind Grand Central Depot—just another Hooverville like one might find anywhere else. Houston's was complete with railroad special agents who prowled the tracks at night and were more than ready to stick a gun into a hobo's ribs and pull the trigger if the bum was trying to freeload a ride back home.[132]

The coroner's inquest books show a marked increase in suicides in the early 1930s, too. They are sad stories mixed in among the other violence: a son gunning down his father in a downtown barbershop, a stabbing among barbecue joint patrons on Runnels Street, a spurned suitor shooting his would-be girl on the mezzanine of the Rice Hotel and a café cook cutting his co-worker to death for leaving crumbs on a prep table. In the spring and summer of 1931, as Houston's bankers were negotiating to bail one another out of any difficulties, there came a spate of tender suicide notes from those who were convinced that their desperate exit would be a selfless sacrifice rather than selfish abandonment of their loved ones.[133]

The deceased, mostly middle-aged men, all cited financial straits, and their acts and messages were painstakingly thoughtful. Emmit Dismuke checked into room 953 at the Rice Hotel before he offed himself with carbolic acid and chloroform so that his wife wouldn't have to find him in their home on Sul Ross.[134]

William A. Davis said he had mismanaged his money and left instructions for the couple who owned his rooming house to give his trunk of belongings to his beneficiary, a young lady from Florida. Davis also told the Van Horns, "It has been a pleasure to me to have the privilege [*sic*] of living or rooming with people that is pleasant and kind." He apologized for "committing the act here," and then he shot himself in the head.

Sixty-two-year-old railroad conductor O.S. Allen wrote his suicide note in July 1930 but waited until St. Patrick's Day 1931 to walk into his garage, lay down a tarpaulin and pull the trigger on his .38 Colt. He even wrote an addendum to the note, starting with "my respite is over," and included instructions for the funeral home and an itemized list of his debts weighed against his $1,000 union life insurance policy.

Allen's letter was as pragmatic as it gets. Having outlived his usefulness and having no prospects, he left advice to his wife of thirty-six years. "I suggest sale of the home," he wrote. "Make it a bargain for cash, then rent a cheaper place and use the money to live on." As to his final wishes, he specified no flowers and "no preaching." Allen also asked that relatives not be notified and that no one tell his son until he would be in town on vacation anyway. In other words, don't make a special trip.[135]

Willis Bridges was fifty-three when he went out to a cut-off road between Airline and East Montgomery and shot himself in the chest that spring. He left a watch, a ring, forty-five cents and two notes for his wife, Em, hoping that she could forgive him and explaining that he was taking this final step since they were "on the verge of starvation," and he couldn't "stand to see [her] suffer or in want." He closed by writing that he "would rather take this step than get a living dishonestly." Other Texans shared no such aversion to a dishonest living.[136]

6
BONNIE AND CLYDE IN HOUSTON— OR NOT

For some down-on-their-luck folks, one escape from hard times was to live vicariously through the exploits of the bank robbers who populated the crime reports and the Federal Bureau of Investigation's Most Wanted list. In the South, and Texas especially, no criminals attracted romantic fascination like Bonnie Parker and Clyde Barrow. The fact is, though, that Barrow had started his life of crime years before any stock market crash. Like the rest of the public enemies, Clyde Barrow was no Robin Hood stealing from the banking blackguards who were foreclosing on hardworking Americans. He was a murdering sociopath, and so were those in the loose confederation that formed his gang.

Barrow was born in Ellis County, just south of Dallas, and it was with childhood acquaintances from the slums of West Dallas, an area known as the Devil's Back Porch and avoided by the law, that he forged his closest bonds. Virtually none of the scores of books on Bonnie and Clyde make much of a tie to Houston. In spite of that, a few stories persist that Clyde Barrow got his start on crime in the Bayou City.

Most of the connections between Barrow's rap sheet and Houston hinge on his occasional membership in the Root Square Gang. The gang was a confederation of low-level teenage criminals who congregated at Root Square Park downtown. In the gang's heyday of the late 1920s, the park was new, having been donated by the family of Houston banker A.P. Root and his wife, Laura, the daughter of his First National banking mentor, B.A. Shepherd. When the couple died, the city block that had held their confection of a Victorian home was given to the city. The park is still there, across La Branch Street from Toyota Center, but today it's more likely to draw urban hoopsters and Rockets fans.[137]

In 1928 and '29, the budding toughs who haunted the square were working their way up the criminal ladder. Aside from the truancy, their early accomplishments included stealing car tires and bicycles. Soon, they graduated to taking the entire auto, and by 1929, certain Root Square boys had a reputation for snatching small safes from garages and repair shops and opening them with nitroglycerine. Following the payoffs from their robberies, the young toughs would spend the evenings at the park, where "there would be a hot dice game after the fellows got drunk and hopped up on 'weed.'" Derill "Dapper Dan" Black, slightly older than most of the others and already married, was a leader. Other names included Jimmie Arnold, Marion Stanley and Johnny Dew. Another name ties Root Square to the soon-to-be-famous Clyde Barrow, though.[138]

When Clyde was still a teenager, he became fast friends with a young man he met in the Dallas lockup, a small-time burglar named Frank "Frenchy" Clause. St. Louis–born Clause had lived in Houston for a time and attended Austin Elementary School on St. Emanuel Street. He also knew "Dapper Dan" Black. It was Clause who brought his friend Barrow to Houston. The crossover between the Bayou City and Big D likely developed because it seemed easy to steal a car in one city and unload it in the other. In spite of the intense dislike that Clyde's mother, Cumie, had for Frank Clause, the primary reason that Clause and Barrow quit hanging out together was that by spring of 1930, Clyde was in jail in Waco, and Frank was in jail in Houston.[139]

Among the several crimes at which teenage Dallasite Clyde Barrow got caught were thefts committed in Fort Worth, Waco and Hillsboro. Ranging a bit farther afield for fertile pickings was not surprising.

During Bonnie and Clyde's two-year run of mayhem, quotes appeared from a former member of the Root Square Gang who refused to give his name. This man, less than twenty-five years old and an unwilling guest at the Harris County Jail, according to the reporter who interviewed him, claimed that Barrow's very first armed robbery was when he joined gang members to knock over a gambling joint in Fort Bend County. Clyde's Saturday Night Special didn't even work. Whether the tale is true or not is tough to judge given the teller's anonymity.[140]

As far as we know from the existing record, the Root Square Gang contented itself with simple felonies until the start of July 1929. On the second of that month, about half past ten o'clock on a sticky Saturday night,

Charles "Buster" Gouge and his eighteen-year-old girlfriend, Lillian Bissett, were enjoying the view and each other along the bayside at Morgan's Point. It was crowded there on the beach—at least two dozen other people were nearby, several at the little refreshment stand and some in the moonlit water, but most utilizing the trysting spot as it was intended.

According to Bissett, someone ran up to where she and Gouge were sitting on a cushion in front of the car and fired a virtually point-blank shot at each of them before quickly vanishing into the dark. Gouge raised himself from the sand and stumbled around briefly before he collapsed. A blaring car horn and the girl's screams got the attention of the wooers and surf gazers. Slowly, a handful of beachgoers ran to her, but for the most part, people skedaddled. Within minutes after the shootings, the point was nearly deserted, the many lovers having started their cars and headed down the road to La Porte.[141]

Among those rushing to help was Mrs. N.A. Segall, who ran the cold drink stand. She hung back until she was certain the gunfire had stopped, but upon arriving she found a stunned Miss Bissett, shot in the abdomen and still somewhat unsure about what had taken place. Buster Gouge lay dead on the sand, the small-caliber bullet having entered one armpit and exited the other, passing through his heart along the way.

After the initial rumors of a peeping Tom or a spurned lover died away, the police were left with nothing to go on. The case dropped from the headlines and languished for nine months, "relegated to the limbo of unsolved crimes." Away from reporters, district attorney's investigator Jimmy Wyatt kept digging, and everything he unearthed led straight to Root Square.[142]

By late March 1930, a circumstantial case had been amassed against Frank Clause and Clyde Barrow. At the time the charges hit, Clause was in jail in Dallas and soon to be transferred to Houston for questioning. Barrow was jailed in Waco, awaiting transfer to the state's Eastham Prison Farm to start a fourteen-year sentence for robbery. From his cell, Clyde emphatically told reporters that he had nothing to do with it. At the time of the Gouge murder, he had been working a legitimate job at the United Glass Company in Dallas.

The cold case warmed when Wyatt and Harris County sheriff T.A. Binford noticed that a string of car burglaries at Morgan's Point had stopped the night of the shootings. The theory that Gouge spooked someone who was messing with his car held much more water than the spurned lover premise, and Harris County lawmen logged several out-of-town trips to interview potential witnesses, many of whom were already scattered among out-of-town jails.

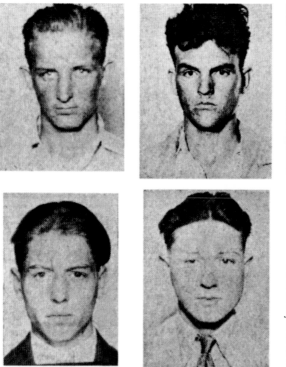

Primary figures in the Buster Gouge killing. *Clockwise from top left*: Jimmie Arnold, Marion Stanley, Dapper Dan Black, Clyde Barrow and Frank Clause. *From the Harris County Archives.*

The names of Barrow and Clause came from Johnny Dew, who was cooling his heels in the Monroe, Louisiana hoosegow, awaiting federal time for car theft. Pressed for names, Dew rolled on the two Dallas associates rather than implicate his closer friends from the Square. The trouble for him was that it took only a few days to confirm both the Clause and Barrow alibis and uncover the fact that Johnny Dew was one of at least four Root Square boys who actually were on Morgan's Point beach the night of July 2.[143]

Rose Cermack, a waitress at Mack's Root Beer Stand, about a mile and a half from Morgan's Point, recalled seeing the youths trade for a .25-caliber pistol that night, the same type of weapon used on Gouge and Bissett. Under some grilling, Dapper Dan admitted that he saw it, too. The purchaser was Jimmie Arnold, Johnny Dew's best friend. The two roomed together at 2204 La Branch, stole cars together and even wore each other's clothes. When Houston reporters, investigator Wyatt and Sheriff Binford traipsed back to Ouachita Parish, Dew finally admitted that Barrow and Clause were not the guys, but that was all Johnny was saying.[144]

The guns from the Buster Gouge killing, booked into evidence. *From the Houston Metropolitan Research Center, Houston Public Library.*

He didn't need to say much more because Marion Stanley busted open like a rotten melon. Stanley and Arnold left Dew that July night to prowl the cars on the beach. As Stanley turned his attention to one auto, he saw Arnold creep through the bushes to Gouge's vehicle. Seconds later, two shots sounded, and Jimmie Arnold ran back saying, "I played hell."

Marion Stanley, Dapper Dan Black and Lillian Bissett all repeated their stories in court. As Arnold was being indicted, the Harris County grand jury no-billed Barrow and Clause. They had dodged the murder charge even if they were each still headed to prison. It wasn't Clyde's first murder, as some have mistakenly claimed, but it was the first time that a major Texas newspaper would run the name Clyde Barrow in a front-page headline.[145]

Jimmie Arnold would never stand trial for the murder of Buster Gouge. The following summer, just starting a seven-year stretch at the state's Clemens Prison Farm near Brazoria, twenty-year-old Arnold died of heat stroke.[146]

When Bonnie and Clyde met their end, their smallish bodies blown apart by six lawmen in Bienville Parish, Louisiana, in May 1934, Houston newspapers ran scads of reminiscences from locals who knew Clyde back in the day—five years earlier. Like everything else connected to Bonnie and Clyde, however, separating fact from legend is just shy of impossible. Were the interview subjects telling the truth or simply angling to get their names in the paper? Or were they confusing the famous Clyde Barrow with another incorrigible Houstonian?

In March 1918, the juvenile court judge in Houston, based on a complaint from probation officer R.R. Adcock, declared Clyde Barrow a delinquent and an incorrigible who had burglarized a house in his own neighborhood. The judge sentenced him to live at the Harris County Home for Boys. The trouble is that the famous Clyde Barrow was not quite nine years old at the time, and by all credible accounts, he was living outside Dallas. In spite of holes in the logic that are big enough to grab Neil Tyson's attention, there remain published accounts that insist the two Clyde Barrows are one and the same.[147]

The 1920 census shows a Clyde Barrow, age sixteen, living with his widowed mother, Eva, in a duplex on Center Street in Houston. Two years prior, Eva Barrow was at 1121 Columbia in the Heights. That information squares with an AP story filed from Houston on the day Bonnie and Clyde were ambushed and killed. "Neighbors in Houston Heights" recalled Clyde as a boy who "would break a bird's wing and laugh loudly at its attempt to fly," the story read. They added that he "got into trouble with several families for torturing their animal pets."[148]

There was no doubt that Clyde Barrow of the Heights was a sadistic scalawag. It's just that he wasn't the Clyde Barrow who made national headlines. How often the two got confused in the public record is impossible to know. Federal census records list at least five boys named Clyde Barrow scattered around Texas in the 1910s and '20s. Sharing such a notorious name as they all became young men must have been a mixed blessing. It might have been particularly difficult in Houston, where the famous Clyde Barrow did make an occasional appearance.[149]

The mingling of myth and reality runs throughout the stories of most all American outlaws, and few had more myth than Bonnie and Clyde. On any given day, newspapers from Alpine, Texas, to Valdosta, Georgia, to Bay City, Michigan, might each run a definitive account of a local man who, with knees knocking, leaned into the window of a Model A Ford and gave directions to the desperadoes.

In truth, the Clyde Barrow Gang members were rather pathetic robbers. They preferred knocking over gas stations to holding up banks, but they excelled at the sadistic serial killing of policemen, gunning down over a dozen. Even some of the small holdup jobs they did pull off went awry, but sensational media coverage promoting a sexy young couple who stole from the man was lapped up by the American public. They were media stars, and they played to it.

In Houston, tales survive of Bonnie and Clyde robbing Citizens State Bank on Washington Avenue (today's Rockefeller's) in 1931 after filling up at a gas station at Waugh and Welch. It is possible that these legends had roots deep in the bottom of a Lone Star bottle that was popped open at Rudyard's across the street from where the allegedly infamous petrol pumps once sat. Facts certainly don't support the story. There have been many books that chronicle the exploits of the outlaw lovebirds, and none includes a credible account of the duo knocking over any joint in Houston. For the record, Clyde spent 1931 incarcerated at the Eastham Prison Farm near Lovelady, Texas.

During their two-year run of mayhem that started upon his early release in February 1932, Bonnie and Clyde were spotted more times than Elvis' ghost at a Dairy Queen. In American history, only Jesse James and perhaps John Dillinger were the subject of as much outlaw legend.

Dillinger, a committed midwesterner, was, in fact, reported to be in Houston at one point. R.B. Delhart told Houston police that two men in a maroon sedan picked him and his wife up on the Airline Road near Humble and dropped them at Airline and 25th Street. There was a Thompson sub-machine gun in the car, Delhart said, and the sandy-haired fellow in the brown fedora had whittled out a toy pistol and introduced himself as Dillinger. In spite of the absence of any related leads, HPD conducted a "vigorous search."[150]

Bonnie and Clyde were Texas regulars, though, so spotting them in Lone Star locales was not so far-fetched. A May 1933 report came in that a man and a woman resembling the pair were spotted in a "bullet-marked automobile" at 8th Street and Heights Boulevard. In December of that year, R.C. Hasty, a Waller man who was hitchhiking, was picked up by a couple in a current-model Chevy coupe. The two asked Hasty to drive them into Houston since the man in the car was nursing an injured arm. Upon being dropped off on Washington Avenue just after midnight, Hasty alerted police to his suspicions since he saw bloodstains, two shotguns and a .45-caliber pistol.[151]

In January 1934, following the Eastham prison break engineered by Barrow, reports came in from around Houston. Filling station owner E.P. Shook reported that a drunken Clyde Barrow stopped for gas at his place on the Airline Road about three o'clock in the morning after the breakout. Though he was alone in the coupe that matched the getaway car, "a larger machine with several men followed him." Police determined that Shook's description of the outlaw "did not coincide with official records."[152]

At the exact same time in Gonzales, fifteen area lawmen, including several from San Antonio and Seguin, surrounded a tourist camp with machine guns, rifles and tear gas, certain they had cornered Bonnie and Clyde. They nearly scared to death the carnival worker and his wife who were the actual occupants of the cabin.[153]

Back in Houston at noon that same day, Sam Brosig called the coppers to say that Barrow and the wanted coupe had driven past Sam's home in the 2400 block of Chenevert. Once again, police found nothing further. After the real getaway car was found in a ravine near Hugo, Oklahoma, many of the lawmen returned "to their homes to await further developments."[154]

Finding the escape car didn't mean finding Barrow and the escapees, however, and it didn't end the Houston-related sightings. By early April 1934, the slightest tip brought swift action. Once again, a gas station attendant sounded the alarm, this time near Manor, just east of Austin. Lawmen closed in to search for two cars carrying two couples and what was believed to be machine guns. Austin police chartered a pair of airplanes. It was believed that the automobiles had sped east on the main highway to Houston, but they got away. Harris County lawmen went into high gear. A motorist near Clinton reported that Clyde passed him on the highway in a tan-colored coupe. The April 6 newspaper also carried reports of Bonnie and Clyde spottings in Kaufman County, Tyler, Wise County and Nacogdoches. That same day, Clyde mortally wounded a constable in the northeast corner of Oklahoma.

Other stories from Highlands in Harris County and over into Chambers County to the east tell of Clyde Barrow stopping by to hide out with relatives when it seemed a suitable spot to lay low. Census records show that the area is filled with Barrows, and unlike some ethereal sightings, there is even a family photograph that supposedly places Bonnie and Clyde in the eastern outskirts of Houston. In the early 1930s, it was just the sort of sleepy backwater they might have sought. Part of what makes these Chambers County stories so alluring is that throughout their months on the lam, the gang made a habit of swinging by to visit relatives, even when authorities were watching.

Yet most deep Southeast Texas historians and genealogists who have checked into the Barrows of Chambers County find no link to Clyde Barrow's family, at least not a close one. Clyde's father, Henry B. Barrow, was born in Alabama and lived in north Florida before coming to Texas, and the Chambers County Barrows can brag about their roots that date to Mexican Texas. Family members and even a descendant of the county sheriff at the time say that while the romance of the tales is interesting, they've never heard a whit of credible evidence that the outlaw couple came there. So this is one Bonnie and Clyde tale seemingly without a smoking gun.[155]

Along with a media that would write anything to sell papers and an abundance of individual fame seekers willing to oblige them, the other part of the equation that makes it tough to discern the truth about Bonnie and Clyde is the simple fact that during much of their two-plus years of fame, they were actively trying to hide. On the other hand, one of the most persistent stories from Southeast Texas is that Bonnie and Clyde stopped into Layl's Root Beer Stand on Highway 90 in Liberty not once, but several times. So if it wasn't a hideout bringing them to the area, maybe it was the burgers.

A NEW NUMBER ONE

There are no known crimes that place Bonnie and Clyde in Houston, but they came close. On August 18, 1932, the duo got in a shooting dustup in Wharton County. The sheriff there, J.C. Willis, wrote to Dallas requesting photographs of the outlaws and explaining that "some of our boys had a little fun with that bunch last night. They took two shots at one of our Deputies." The gang would become less fun for lawmen over the next several months.[156]

Perhaps Houston's biggest brushes with the Barrow Gang came not from Parker and Barrow themselves but courtesy of Raymond Hamilton, a swaggering braggart of an outlaw killer who was alternately part of and a rival to Clyde's gang. He and Clyde had taken part in the shooting of two sheriff's deputies at the Stringtown Dance Hall in Oklahoma in 1932, and he was with them when they ran afoul of deputies in Wharton County. It was Hamilton who was the primary prize in the famous January 1934 jailbreak Barrow orchestrated at Eastham Prison Farm, where he'd been incarcerated himself. Clyde had arranged for Hamilton and fellow inmate Joe Palmer to obtain two .45 automatic pistols that had been hidden in a woodpile on the farm. One guard was killed and another was wounded in the escape, and two other opportunistic prisoners came with them.

Raymond Hamilton, like Clyde Barrow, was a physically small man, standing only five feet, three inches tall—two inches shorter than Clyde. Bonnie was a good fit for the gang at only about four feet, eleven inches. Not surprisingly, there was little formal education there either. Writings from all the male members of the gang were rife with misspellings. Sometimes they didn't even come close.

Hamilton's breakup with the gang came at the start of March 1934 and was sealed via such a letter postmarked from the Lafayette Hotel in New

Orleans to his Dallas attorney in which he distanced himself from Clyde. Ray considered himself a gentleman bandit, and most assuredly one who was above the small-time gas station stickups that marked much of the Barrow Gang's work. It set off an exchange of angry public statements from Barrow and Hamilton. Each time, the letter or telegram was marked with a fingerprint to show that the missive was "on the level."[157]

Hamilton denied killing anyone, claiming that he hadn't been with the Barrow Gang "since the Lanster Bank Robbery." That robbery was a $4,000 theft in Lancaster near Dallas. Clyde responded with a fiery and contradictory telegram. He claimed Hamilton was "too dum to know how to put a clip in a automatic," and said that it made him "sick to see a yellow punk like that playing baby."

Unlike Clyde, Ray Hamilton enjoyed holing up around Houston. The Bayou City was his alibi when Barrow and Henry Methvin gunned down two motorcycle cops in Grapevine on Easter Sunday 1934. After numerous reports from around the state placed him with Bonnie and Clyde in a Ford V-8 with yellow wire wheels, Ray wrote the Lafayette Hotel letter to make sure authorities knew that he was hiding out in Houston at the time.

"I was in Houston Wednesday, April 4," wrote Hamilton. "And have been here (New Orleans) since Thur. even. April 5."[158]

The public statement worked but was hardly necessary. The Grapevine killings were pinned squarely on Clyde Barrow, but part of the reason was the rather ironclad evidence that placed Hamilton in Houston a couple of days prior.

On March 31, the day before Easter, Raymond, accompanied by his girlfriend, Mary O'Dare, robbed a bank in West, Texas, of $1,900. The woman was the wife of an old criminal partner of Hamilton's, a man who was serving a ninety-nine-year sentence. Aside from Raymond, nobody seemed to think much of her. She had been working as a prostitute until Ray picked her up in Amarillo. His brother, Floyd Hamilton, described her as a "short girl with plenty of curves and a hard face covered by enough makeup to grow a crop." It was Mary who had been a chief catalyst for Hamilton leaving the Barrow Gang in the first place, helping Ray steal money from the group's haul and suggesting to Bonnie that she dump Clyde. On top of every other complaint against her, she couldn't drive.[159]

When Raymond Hamilton came running from the State National Bank in the town of West, Mary O'Dare was behind the wheel of the getaway car. She made it only a few miles before she ran the car through a ditch, knocking herself out in the process and breaking Ray's nose.[160]

The first to happen along was Mrs. Cam Gunter of Mexia, who was passing by with her four-year-old son, Jolly. When she stopped to render aid, Hamilton pulled his gun, booted the young boy out of the car and told Mrs. Gunter to head south. They arrived in Houston around sunup, but not before the machine gun–toting Hamilton pulled off into some woods near Conroe and allowed the two women to catch some sleep. Mrs. Gunter told HPD that she had been treated "nicely." Hamilton left his kidnap victim with thirty dollars "to have her car fixed up." After posing in hammy pictures for news photographers, including one in which she held a machine gun, Mrs. Gunter returned to Mexia and her family. One of the next times she made the newspaper was when her grown-up son Jolly got married in Corpus Christi.[161]

Needing a new car in Houston, Raymond Hamilton snagged a black Ford V-8 sedan with yellow wire wheels—remarkably similar to the one Clyde was driving when he and accomplice Methvin gunned down the two highway patrolmen at Grapevine. The owner of the car, Clyde Clayton of 413 Woodland Avenue, was walking into his mother's house a few blocks away to give her an Easter bouquet. He did get his car back, but not until Hamilton had put almost 1,600 miles on it in five days' time. Ray was thoughtful enough to drive it back to the Gulf Coast, though. Police found it, the inside soaked with rain, on Allendale Road near the Shell Refinery.[162]

As the clock ran out on Barrow and Parker, Ray Hamilton's criminal star brightened; if the goal was notoriety, that placed a bigger target on his back. There was one minor setback to be weathered. Raymond Hamilton was captured after he and a "chance companion" robbed a bank at Lewisville. Sporting over 360 years of prison sentence, Ray went back into the system, this time on death row.[163]

Raymond heard about the killing of the famous Bonnie and Clyde while he was cooling his heels in Huntsville. It was there, only days after the ambush, that Hamilton received a letter written in Bonnie's hand and signed by Clyde. In it, Barrow offered enmity instead of sympathy and wrote that he'd been looking for Hamilton with the intent to kill him, something that should have happened earlier. Barrow also added that when he busted Raymond out of Eastham, Ray was not the changed man he expected, just the same "boastful punk."[164]

Not quite two months later, Hamilton would finally become the most wanted man in Texas. On the afternoon of July 22, 1934, the vast majority of inmates at the Walls were in the stadium watching their beloved Prison Tigers baseball team battle the semi-pro powerhouse Humble Oilers. A tough habitual criminal named Charlie Frazier and the aptly paired Whitey

Walker and Blackie Thompson had picked this time for an escape, and Hamilton and former Barrow Gang member Joe Palmer came with them. Walker didn't make it, but the other three busted out of the death house and onto the front pages.[165]

The author of several of those front-page articles was the chain-smoking, foul-mouthed crusading crime reporter for the *Houston Press*, a man named Harry McCormick, or Mack to his friends. He did more than just tell the stories of criminals. In an era when Texas prison corruption was rampant and brutality was such that a guard murdering an inconvenient inmate was not particularly out of the ordinary, McCormick and his editors, Marcellus Foster and Royal Roussel, were the top journalists in the state, railing for reform. It gave Mack a street cred that was known throughout the Texas underworld, nowhere more so than among former members of the Barrow Gang.[166]

Houston Press crime reporter Harry McCormick. *From the Houston Metropolitan Research Center, Houston Public Library.*

At the start of the 1930s, McCormick penned a series of exposés about the prison system, with much of his information passed along via a prison chaplain and fellow Houstonian, Father Hugh Finnegan, a man who would accompany well over one hundred condemned men on their last walks. Among the inmates at Eastham who were funneling information to Harry were Ralph Fults, Raymond Hamilton and Clyde Barrow. Mack considered Fults and Hamilton to be his friends, though he laughed out loud when Raymond told him that he'd bust out of the Huntsville death house and give Harry an interview.[167]

In fact, Harry's acquaintance with state and local criminals went back even before 1930. He came to Houston from the *Denver Post* in the late 1920s and would remain in the city for a decade. Among his early haunts in search of a good seedy lead was Root Square.

In that hectic, bloody Easter week that started April 1934, when Clyde Barrow and Henry Methvin were murdering the two highway patrolmen and Raymond Hamilton was robbing a bank and bringing his hostage to Houston, Harry McCormick received an anonymous letter at his office in the *Houston Press* building on Rusk. It included a crudely drawn map to a spot on the Texas-Louisiana border and gave details of the abuses happening at Eastham. It also promised that if Mack followed the map, he'd find one of Texas prison boss "Lee Simmons' chief rats."[168]

McCormick, the trusted advocate of prison reform, followed the story to Shreveport, where he and law officers began chasing the clues on the map. It led them to the once-well-dressed body of a man, a body that had been there for three or four days. His skull had been crushed, and he sported several gunshot wounds. In his pocket were sixteen dollar bills and "three pair of crooked dice."

It didn't take long to identify the man as W.H. McNabb, an inmate trustee from Eastham. From there, it took a bit longer for the pieces to present a full picture of what happened. Not until Ralph Fults told the story decades later would the final details emerge, and their roots lay in the rule of thumb that it's never good to be weak in prison.[169]

Joe Palmer suffered badly from asthma and other respiratory trouble. His frequent incapacitation was the thing that drove Raymond Hamilton to want Joe out of the Barrow Gang so badly he once pointed a gun at Joe's head while he slept in the back seat of a speeding getaway car. At the Eastham Prison Farm, one guard and one trustee building tender were particularly thorough at beating Palmer to a pulp when he was too sick for work detail. Palmer shot and killed the offending guard when he busted out of Eastham, and now he was after the trustee. It was something Palmer was not about to let go.[170]

Two months before the anonymous letter to McCormick, in his last act before taking a break from the gang, Barrow had driven Palmer to Houston, where he could pay an attorney to spread some cash around Huntsville to get McNabb a furlough. Such practices were common for the most trusted inmates.

Palmer's plan worked perfectly. On March 29, W.H. McNabb disappeared from a domino parlor in Gladewater, Texas, near the start of his sixty-day furlough. Barrow, who had killed his own bully at Eastham, a big con who was repeatedly raping the diminutive Barrow, was there to lend Palmer an empathetic hand. The next time anyone saw McNabb was in the muddy pasture just a handful of yards into Texas, and just as Palmer and Barrow had hoped, Harry McCormick made certain that the world got their message.[171]

Raymond Hamilton also had people he could trust in Houston, and not just Harry McCormick. Days after robbing the Beaumont National Guard Armory of eight Browning Automatic Rifles in February 1935, Hamilton dumped a getaway car near where the Barker–Clodine Road crossed Buffalo Bayou. Police towed it into Houston for examination. Once again, "possible hiding places" were searched to no avail.[172]

Harris County Sheriff's Department fingerprint experts went over the car, finding evidence of three people, none of whom was Raymond Hamilton. One was, however, Estelle Davis, a young Houston woman with a long rap sheet that even included moonshining. She and her older sister, Dorothy, had a predilection for running with convicts and fugitives. Perhaps it was genetic. Their brother, Dan T. Davis, had been on multiple holdups. One was in Cleveland, Texas, in January 1933 and included Estelle and Dorothy. Older sister Beryl Davis Kearns was also a jailhouse regular. (Beryl missed out when her three siblings were indicted for the holdup in Liberty County.)

Dorothy and Estelle—or Dot and Stella, as most called them—had hooked up with a whole string of desperadoes. Stella had even been married to one, "Baby Face" Earl Joiner, who had robbed the same First National Bank in Cleveland the previous fall. After the January Cleveland bank heist, which included a full-on, downtown gunfight with local townspeople, newspapers reported that Stella and her sister were the "actual brains of the operation." Unlike her less-brainy cohorts, Stella did manage to elude authorities for several days.[173]

Their ties to Hamilton went back to at least his escape from the death house. It had been the Davis sisters who worked as intermediaries for Charlie

Frazier, the mastermind of the escape and a convict who was sporting lead from two previous attempts to check out of Huntsville early. Frazier had also been involved, and wounded, in a successful prison break at Angola in Louisiana that included Stella's husband, Earl.

Louisiana lawmen alleged that Stella and Dot had already engineered successful jailbreaks at Marksville, Alexandria and Shreveport. For the Huntsville break, the women delivered $500 cash and three .45 pistols to prison guard Jim Patterson at a local café. They also drove the two black Ford getaway cars that sped Hamilton, Thompson and Palmer—the only convicts to make it out that day—away from the southwest corner of the Walls.[174]

Palmer was captured in Kentucky only three weeks later, and Thompson went out in the proverbial hail of bullets in Amarillo, but Hamilton's run lasted longer. The Davis sisters, who sometimes used the name of their hometown of Houston as an alias, stayed in touch.

They also became close to Harry McCormick after they called his office one day from a drugstore on McKinney to say they had a letter from Charlie Frazier. Mack befriended the sisters over the next few months, serving as their taxi, buying them beer and taking them for meals at the drive-in.

On Monday, March 18, 1935, roughly a month after dumping the Beaumont armory car, Raymond Hamilton and Ralph Fults stopped at a sandwich stand in the Heights to tell a waitress that they wanted to talk to her sisters. Modelle Davis was no stranger to the circles in which Stella and Dot ran. That evening, one of the Davis girls called Harry McCormick's home phone and cryptically told him to come take the sisters out, but first they needed to "pick up five chicken dinners." Mack drove to the corner of 11th and Shepherd, arriving in about twenty minutes.[175]

As he pulled to a stop, Dot Davis jumped in beside him and said, "Tail my sister." They headed west on 11th Street and then sped northwest on Hempstead Highway. Around the little community of Satsuma, the lead car turned down a dirt road, pulled over the railroad tracks and flashed its lights to another vehicle. McCormick walked to the third vehicle and slid into the back seat next to Raymond Hamilton, the most wanted man in Texas. Belying the automatic rifle on his lap and the small arsenal on the seat, Hamilton doffed his hat as he said hello. The time had come for his promised interview.[176]

Fults pulled away with Stella behind him and Dot bringing up the rear of the caravan in McCormick's car. "It's not safe to hang around in one place for too long," said Hamilton.

The rolling interview continued all the way to Hempstead, where the three cars turned north onto Highway 6. Along the way, Fults and Hamilton spilled the beans about the death-house escape and the ambush in McKinney a few weeks earlier that had almost ended their lives. They made it clear that Harry could use the stories as needed, but everyone agreed to leave any mention of the two Davis sisters out of the telling. Hamilton wanted "the people of Texas to know" his side of the story—he'd never killed anybody. Finally, there was the real crux of the visit: giving Harry $2,000 to pass to Joe Palmer's lawyer.

"We hope it'll buy a stay of execution," Ray told him. "It's the least we can do."

Around 4:30 a.m., in a pasture near the community of Retreat, the outlaw quartet bound and gagged Harry McCormick and carried him back to his own car. They busted out the headlights and cut the wire to the horn. The idea, Hamilton said, was "to keep the feds off you, we best make out like we kidnapped you and held you against your will." Almost twenty-five years later, in a magazine story, McCormick was still distorting the facts to avoid any potential prosecution.[177]

The final act for Raymond Hamilton was to plant a full set of fingerprints on the windshield, dash and hood of Harry's car. Just a few hours later, the four outlaws held up a grocery store in San Antonio.

Harry McCormick's efforts to keep the Davis sisters' names out of the papers were rather futile. Two weeks later, Dorothy and Estelle would be splashed in newsprint across the South, driving the getaway car for Hamilton and Ralph Fults as they robbed a bank in Prentiss, Mississippi. The biggest downside for the two women was that the stories concerned their incarceration in separate cells at the Hinds County Jail in Jackson. Their statement to officers was that they'd been forced to go along with the bandits.[178]

Raymond Hamilton's prison holiday ended not long after the staged McCormick abduction and the run through the mid-South. He was surrounded in a rail yard at Fort Worth on April 5 and gave up without a fight. In the end, he was reunited on death row with Joe Palmer, the man he once plotted to shoot in the head while he slept when the two were still riding with Clyde Barrow's gang.[179]

Deputies in Denton dragged Ralph Fults from a wrecked car less than two weeks after Hamilton's recapture. When they brought him to Huntsville, prison officials came under embarrassing fire from state legislators and the Texas Prison Board over the horrible brutality at the

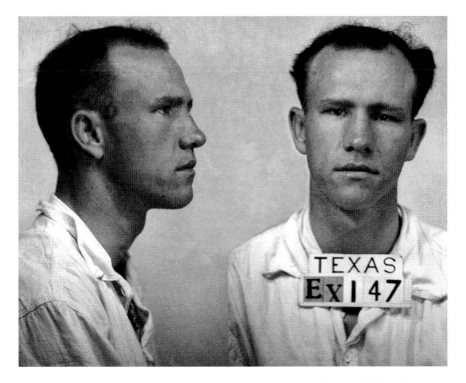

Twenty-two-year-old Raymond Hamilton's execution mug shot. *From the TDCJ Archives.*

Retrieve Farm near Angleton. Convicts faced such abuse that many chopped off their own hands or feet in an attempt to be moved to the prison hospital. Prison manager Lee Simmons' answer to reporters was, "Give them more axes if they need them."[180]

With pressure ratcheted up on the prison bosses, they looked for a scapegoat, and their top target was Harry McCormick, the crusading crime reporter they had already banned from entry into prison facilities. Officials worked on Ralph Fults with a combination of threats and promises. They wanted him to give up Mack for a harboring charge.[181]

"Sure as I'm standing here," Fults told the man. "We kidnapped Harry McCormick."

Joe Palmer and Raymond Hamilton both breathed their last in the Texas electric chair in the first minutes of May 10, 1935. Palmer died first, and then Hamilton "made a brave showing after cracking earlier in the day." Joe Palmer comforted Hamilton, who had lost control that afternoon at the prospect of his death. At the end, twenty-two-year-old Raymond thanked

Father Finnegan and wished him well on his upcoming trip to Ireland. Then he added, "Goodbye to all." Three blasts of electrical current, a "sizzling noise," an eerie screech of the dynamo and a clenching of his hands, and one of the nation's Public Enemies was scratched from the list. Among the witnesses was Harry McCormick.[182]

A LAST GASP

The legend of Bonnie and Clyde didn't start in Houston, but that was where one of the final chapters ended in the person of W.D. "Deacon" Jones. He was born in Henderson, Texas, and raised in the same squalid, extremely poor Trinity River Bottoms of West Dallas that produced Clyde Barrow and blues guitar legend T-Bone Walker. In 1922, Jones was six years old and living in a squatter's camp under the Oak Cliff Viaduct when he met Barrow, who was then twelve years old. Less than a year later, Jones' father, sister and one of his five brothers all perished in a flu epidemic. His mother, Tookie, and four of his brothers survived.[183]

By 1931, the teenage Deacon Jones, a first-grade dropout, was a known police character—a car thief of increasing ability. The next year, on Christmas Eve, Bonnie and Clyde stopped in to see him on their way through Dallas with the police in hot pursuit. The gang had a vacancy. They needed an assistant. Jones signed on, and the very next day, in an attempted car jacking, the gang killed a twenty-seven-year-old Temple, Texas man. Exactly who fired the fatal shot is unknown, but Jones later said that Barrow convinced him that he had done it in order to bind him to the gang. "Boy you can't go home," Jones remembered Barrow telling him. "You got murder on you, just like me." (Jones was indicted but not tried for the murder.)[184]

A few weeks later, Barrow killed a Tarrant County deputy sheriff after the gang was ensnared in a trap set for other criminals. The trio then headed east into Arkansas and Missouri, where they briefly kidnapped a Springfield cop, whom they released, unharmed, six hours later. (They relieved him of his fancy Russian gun. Years later, the cop allowed his daughter to bring him to show-and-tell at her school.)

In March, the gang posed and shot those famous roadside pictures that were later captured by police. April found them heading up Route 66 to Joplin, Missouri, where they killed two cops in another gun battle. Jones took a bullet to the side; Parker used knitting needles to pry open the wound and then dumped rubbing alcohol inside him. Somehow Jones survived.

A few weeks after that, Jones had had enough of the gang life. He escaped from the gang in Ruston, Louisiana, and headed back to Dallas. About six weeks later, Bonnie and Clyde found him there and, in Jones' telling, more or less forced him back in.

More gun battles, more blood, more death. An Arkansas farmer shot off two of Jones' fingertips in one fight. Clyde's brother Buck was killed in another. Bonnie Parker's leg was disfigured after it was burned or scalded with battery acid after a car wreck. The sixteen-year-old Jones wanted out again, for good this time.

In Clarksdale, Mississippi, Barrow told Jones to gas up a car they'd stolen and gave him a couple of bucks. Jones tanked up the car and

Clyde Barrow (left) and W.D. Jones. *From the Dallas Municipal Archives.*

hightailed to Houston, where Tookie had moved. Here, he chopped cotton and picked vegetables and hoped to lay low, but he was betrayed by an acquaintance and turned over to Dallas County lawmen. Deacon Jones spilled like a toddler with a bad sippy cup, giving lawmen all sorts of particulars about the last year's worth of Barrow Gang activities. For the murder of the Tarrant County cop, Jones was sentenced to sixteen years in prison. He served six.[185]

Jones was in the Dallas County Jail when he heard that Bonnie and Clyde had been killed. He told reporters that he was relieved.

After his parole, in or about 1941, Jones moved back to Houston. He tried to volunteer for the army at the onset of World War II, but they would not accept him because of all his wounds. (He also said he was missing a piece of his lung.)

He settled into a quiet life at 1519 Hendricks Street, a little house off Hardy. He lived next door to Tookie for many years. He reportedly became addicted to a concoction of paregoric mixed with Jack Daniel's at some point and spent a few months of the last year of his life in a federal prison after he was caught with three thousand barbiturates. In 1972, he went to county jail for a stretch after forfeiting his bond in a DWI case.

After the 1967 Warren Beatty–Faye Dunaway film came out, Jones was thrust into the spotlight. (Michael J. Pollard's "C.W. Moss" character was partially based on Jones.) He gave an interview to *Playboy*. Some TV reporters took him to a Houston screening at a drive-in. Jones was not impressed. "[It] made it all look sort of glamorous," he said, "but like I told them teenaged boys sitting near me at the drive-in showing: 'Take it from an old man who was there. It was hell.'"[186]

He told *Playboy* that the only scenes that were not "plumb silly" were the gun battles. "Them was real enough to almost make me hurt," he said.

He later unsuccessfully sued the producers, claiming the film had maligned his character by portraying him as a gung-ho, willing participant in the crime spree.

"Deacon" Jones' last gun battle wasn't much of a fight. Unlike in his Depression-era stint in the Barrow Gang, Deacon Jones was not armed this time around.

You could say he was loaded, though—with booze, downers and lead. A machine gun bullet was lodged in his chest, birdshot in his face and buckshot in his chest and arm—all souvenirs of the infamous multi-state crime sprees of his youth.

In the wee hours of August 20, 1974, Jones and a female companion arrived at the Northside home of a man named George Jones. (No relation to Deacon.) Deacon demanded that the woman be allowed to stay for the night. George Jones said no. Deacon restated his desires more forcefully. George Jones responded with three twelve-gauge rejoinders, and Deacon Jones collapsed dead in the driveway with wounds to the groin, armpit and thigh.[187]

George Jones was charged with murder, but the case was later dismissed. He said he feared Deacon's reputation and knew that he was often armed with a knife or gun. George said that Deacon was a nice man when sober, but Deacon was apparently anything but sober on the night he died.

So ended Deacon Jones' life of poverty, infamy, addiction, late notoriety and shame.

Jones is buried at Brookside Memorial Park on the Eastex Freeway.

THE BEATNIK KILLERS
GUN-TORCH MURDERS

Like the rest of America, 1961 Houston was on the cusp of radical, sweeping cultural change, nowhere more so than in Riverside Terrace. A middle-class-to-wealthy enclave hugging Brays Bayou southeast of downtown, Riverside had been developed in the 1920s and '30s in large part for well-heeled Jews who were then barred by covenant from settling in River Oaks, the elite new suburb on the other side of downtown. Along North and South McGregor Streets, families like the Sakowitzes, Battelsteins and Fingers built elegant mansions designed by famous architects, and by the 1960s, the oak trees they planted were throwing ample shade on the sun-dappled backstreets.

South of the commercial strip along Old Spanish Trail and east of Scott Street, just outside Riverside proper, lay blocks and blocks of small two- and three-bedroom starter homes built for World War II veterans, whose sacrifices were honored on the map in one neighborhood, where the streets were given names like Tarawa, Bataan, Anzio and Kasserine Pass. There on busy Griggs Road was the office of Fred A. Tones, realtor, and on February 6, 1961, it would become one of two related crime scenes in the "Gun-Torch Murders" perpetrated by "Beatnik Killers" that would rock the city of Houston and spawn both a true-crime book (Robert Bentley's *Dangerous Games*) and an X-rated B movie.

Fred Tones presented himself as a pillar of the community—a family man, a regular parishioner at St. Peter of the Apostle Church and a Knight of Columbus. He also presented himself as a go-getter, a real live wire of a real estate man. Then forty-four years old, the balding, short, stocky Tones—he stood five feet, four inches tall and weighed in at 150 pounds—was driving a sparkling white 1960 Lincoln Premiere. He specialized in selling his own neighborhood (the welter of streets south of Riverside), and in early 1961, he told a competitor that he was averaging one sale per day. This was very likely a lie, as Riverside and all adjoining areas were in the agonizing process of integration. In 1952, a black cattleman named Jack Ceaser bought a home in Riverside and stayed even after someone planted a bomb on his porch. After that came the blockbusters and white flight. The wealthier Jews at last found acceptance in River Oaks, and those less affluent built a whole new subdivision (Meyerland) several miles west along Brays Bayou.

At any rate, at that particular time, few whites were buying in the Riverside area, and given that the influx of black residents had yet to begin in earnest, Tones' competitor doubted his story. Still, he did have that Lincoln, even if he was trying desperately to sublet a portion of his small office.

Or then again, maybe he did sell all those houses. Maybe his cash-flow problem had a different cause.

Tones' demise was set into motion one morning in late December. Tones was tooling around in his big Lincoln. Ranging afield from his Riverside homestead, he was on Truxillo Street near the old Light Guard Armory building when he first saw Carolyn Lima. The statuesque brunette teen was wearing tight toreador pants and shaking out a dusty carpet on her front porch at 1205 Truxillo Street. (A few years later, the block would be the sight of the Truxillo Arms, the locus of Houston's hard-partying folk and country music scene, where people like Townes Van Zandt and Guy Clark partied and crashed many a night.)[188]

Entranced, Tones slammed on the brakes, backed up his Lincoln and asked if he could take her out for coffee and talk real estate. Lima was already a seasoned prostitute by this time, so she knew the deal when she got in Tones' flashy car. Real estate, hell—here was a trick, one with lots of money. After some perfunctory chat at a nearby drive-in about the neighborhood—Lima's IQ was once measured at 72, and she was seventeen years old—Tones cut to the chase. He wanted to come back to her apartment. Lima agreed and charged him twenty-five dollars, and while they were at it, her roommate, Leslie Douglas Ashley, watched from the shadows, his presence unknown to Tones. After Tones gave Lima his card and left her with the instructions to call whenever she wanted a "date," Lima hopped in the sack for a "French date" (oral sex) with Ashley, a male prostitute with a girl's name who longed to be a woman and who would years later claim—erroneously—to be "Houston's first true drag queen."[189]

These two lovers were both tenth-grade dropouts from hardscrabble backgrounds. Lima's father had abandoned her mother with three children in Houston Heights, a once-genteel but then-decaying (and now genteel again) neighborhood soon to become the sickening playground of serial killers Elmer Wayne Henley and Dean Corll. Ashley was the son of Sylvia Kipperman—from a Jewish Hot Springs, Arkansas family of cobblers—and Leslie Ashley Sr., a louche redneck who went to prison for auto theft and later joined the army. Upon his return from the service, Ashley and Kipperman divorced, and Kipperman moved to Houston to join her only sibling, a brother ten years her senior. She married a man named Ayres, her brother's partner in a photography shop, and they settled into life in a brick bungalow on Wentworth Street, just outside Riverside Terrace.

As Leslie Jr. grew through childhood, he came to realize he was not like most other boys. He loved trying on his mother's dresses. He thought of himself as a sissy. Some speculated than one or more of his babysitters had molested him while his mom was working, supporting the family while his dad was in the army. He frequently ran away from home and was caught by the police turning a bus station trick by the age of twelve. Instead of hunting with his dad—who remained a presence in his life and even bought him a rifle—Leslie preferred to tootle the clarinet in his room. He attempted suicide several times: slashing his wrists, swallowing a handful of pills and filling his room with gas. At the time, nobody considered the option that he was legitimately a woman trapped in a man's body. "That boy ain't right," was pretty much the prevailing opinion on Leslie Douglas Ashley.

Leslie still believed he could force himself into a straight life. As a teen, the tenth-grade dropout married a Mexican-American girl named Rose and moved into her Magnolia Park barrio near the Houston Ship Channel. He even fathered a child by her. Already having a hard time financially and quarreling constantly, the baby added even more strain, and soon their marriage was foundering like a concrete freighter. Many young families face such crises, but the marriage of Leslie and Rose was far more unusual than most. "The difficulty lies in his recreational activities," wrote a Jewish Family Service counselor in a report commissioned by Leslie's mother in a last-ditch effort to save her son's marriage. "He seems drawn to places where queers hang out, and where people are queers. He invites them to his home and he takes her to these places. She has been very upset about this, and this is the greatest reason for their quarrels." Leslie and Rose were soon divorced.

A couple of months later, still grieving the failure of his union, Leslie, then about to turn twenty-three, met the seventeen-year-old Lima at a bar frequented by lesbians, one of several such establishments in Houston's then deeply underground gay underground, albeit one that would be known by the end of the decade as "the homosexual playground of the South."[190] Performing as the Amazing Dynamite Renee "Cookie" LaMonte, Ashley was a regular on the stages at drag bars like the Pink Elephant (at Main and Bell downtown) and the predominantly African Desert Room. And "Cookie" was what Carolyn Lima called Leslie. He made her laugh, and they quickly fell in love.

An aspiring beautician, Lima did Leslie's hair and make-up, and they soon shot enough film of Leslie posing in drag to fill whole scrapbooks. She saw him as her fashion guinea pig and dyed his hair a different color every Saturday night. After they moved in together—telling the dowager landlady they were siblings—Leslie claimed they had incredible sex, with Lima saying that his nude dancing performances to the record player made her laugh as she had never before. The carless couple loved walking to a nearby drugstore, where they spent countless hours at a soda fountain, knocking back Cokes, chowing down on burgers and laughing themselves silly. They filled the Truxillo house with four cats, a fish tank and a poodle named Fifi. Lima had dumped a soldier fiancé by then, and she told her mother she was now engaged to Leslie. It was pretty much a perfect union of two young and damaged souls, marred only by a harsh economic reality that compelled them to cruise Houston's tenderloin picking up tricks, or servicing their most loyal clientele—a horde of horny boys from nearby San Jacinto High School.

This, of course, was how they met Fred Tones, a man who was no stranger to places like the Pink Elephant and the Desert Room himself, albeit only as a spectator and participant in the extracurricular post-closing festivities. An insatiable appetite for sex took the father of three wherever it could be found and to the bed of whomever he could find.

For a few weeks, he was content with his assignations with Lima. One night, he brought a buddy along, and Lima took Cookie—who took his ex-wife's name of Rose for the evening—along to complete a foursome. Nothing happened as the quartet (save for the abstemious Lima) polished off a fifth of hooch, aimlessly driving around the chilly Houston streets. A little later, Tones had sex with Lima in her apartment and found Leslie in the apartment after they were done. This time, Leslie was wearing men's clothes. Lima introduced him as her brother "Douglas," and Tones was none the wiser. The three of them piled into Tones' Lincoln and headed up to the Pig Stand, a pioneering Dallas-based restaurant chain and purveyor of pork barbecue sandwiches. Since it was across town on Washington Avenue, Tones was bold enough to take them inside, and he would take the two of them there several times in the weeks to come.[191]

At some point, Tones figured out that "Rose" and Douglas were one and the same, if he had ever been fooled to begin with. His reaction stunned Lima. He asked if she could bring Douglas along for a three-way session, or "sex party," as the papers would refer it to in the months and years to come. Lima told Tones she would ask her lover, who was not interested in the act but was interested in the money.

Meanwhile, the couple had laid aside enough cash to put down $120 on a $320, 1953 Packard Clipper, a lemon that started falling apart days after their purchase. Worse trouble was around the corner: according to Leslie, one night, some of the San Jacinto High School clientele saw him out of drag and realized that they had been going on French dates with a man. On the evening of February 3, on two separate occasions, carloads of outraged youths screeched to a halt outside 1205 Truxillo Street, broke windows and catcalled and jeered Lima and Leslie. By one estimate, there were as many as twenty boys outside at one time.

On the second occasion, a few of the kids broke in and smashed up the place, including Leslie's beloved kitschy Buddha statues. Leslie and Lima had fled, and a cop later told Lima she needed to buy a gun. Not long afterward, with Leslie's hair a shocking peach-pink hue, they piled in the Packard, headed up to the foot of Main Street, then one of Houston's seediest areas, and bought a fourteen-dollar, .22-caliber, West German–made Eig Saturday night special with a two-inch barrel. For additional protection, they also drove out to the Hobby Airport area to pick up a German shepherd with heartworms that a friend had tipped them to.[192]

Over the next few days, Tones continued pressuring Lima to bring Leslie along on a future date, and Lima kept passing those entreaties along to an ambivalent Leslie. No, he did not want to do what Tones wanted, but he most certainly wanted and needed the money he was offering. That need for money became even more pressing on February 5, when their landlady decided that she did not want the denizens of one of her properties to be sexually servicing the entire male student body of San Jacinto High School's class of 1961. She handed the "siblings" an eviction notice. All that, plus that damn Packard was still playing up, and Tones had left them another note begging for a threesome.

There are winter days in Houston that make you feel like you are living inside a cloud—cold but not bitter, moist but not soaking. Some kind of wetness is falling from the sky, and it feels like barely melted sleet. February 6, 1961, the last day of Fred Tones' life, was just such a day.

As his wife got their kids to school, he put on his Sears suit, pulled on his Nunn-Bush shoes, screwed on his happy face, jump-started his live-wire attitude and drove his Lincoln the two blocks to his failing office. He was there by 9:00 a.m. and called his wife around noon from somewhere that was not the office. He returned there around 2:30 p.m. By the time Tones arranged an early evening date with Lima, Leslie had decided that they needed the twenty-five dollars enough for him to at least just go along with the proceedings for the time being. He rode to Tones' office alongside Lima, who generally did most of the driving. The Packard died again, this time in the driveway.

Though they had been told no other employees would be at Fred Tones Realty when they arrived in the five o'clock gloom, Gutierrez, Tones' secretary, was still there doing the books, while Tones was talking on the phone. Gutierrez told them to be seated in the waiting area while her boss yakked away. When he hung up, she went in to tell him a young couple was waiting to see him. Gutierrez then left the trio alone but had difficulty in easing her car around the disabled Packard out back.

Exactly what happened a few minutes later at the Griggs Road sex party is not up for debate: Carolyn Lima emptied that little .22 she had just purchased into Fred Tones in his own office. And then she and Leslie trundled his half-nude body into the trunk of his Lincoln, drove it to a godforsaken drainage ditch in an industrial section of the Magnolia Park barrio, doused it in gasoline and set it on fire. So much for the what, where and when. How and why it happened—self-defense or cold-blooded murder—would be for the courts to decide, not once but twice; of course, only two of the participants were available to give their renditions.

Though they had been spotted by one of Tones' neighbors—a University of Houston pharmacy student who knew them by name and sight from their drugstore canoodlings—and though police had their pictures and knew they were driving Tones' Lincoln, it took three weeks to nab the duo. After torching Tones' corpse, they enjoyed a sort of bizarro honeymoon. Using Tones' cash, they barreled first to Galveston and then east to the Big Easy, where they reveled at Mardi Gras for a few days. Next, they headed north to New York's Hell's Kitchen, an area Leslie had known and loved back in his teenage-runaway prostitute days. That was where the FBI found them in late February. Leslie was apprehended in drag. By March, they were back in Houston and facing charges of capital murder. Harris County district attorney Frank Briscoe was swinging for the fences with this case. If convicted, Lima and Leslie would be heading for the Walls in Huntsville and an imminent date with the Texas electric chair.[193]

While Houston does lie in the Bible Belt, it was also known as a "whiskey and trombone town." That about sums up the trial of Lima and Leslie, the "Beatnik Killers," as they were known in the old scandal-sheet *Houston Press*. Judge Miron Love's courtroom was packed to the rafters daily with gawkers who had fought their way in to hear the kinky, X-rated testimony firsthand. Jack Knight represented the defendants jointly, and his strategy centered on exposing Fred Tones' unsavory dark side. Judge Love disallowed all but the barest hints of Tones' bad character, and Knight's defense sank like a lead balloon. Leslie Douglas Ashley and Carolyn Lima were convicted and condemned to dates with Old Sparky. At the time, it was believed that only one woman—an alleged robber and axe murderess called Chipita Rodriguez, whose name was cleared in the 1980s—had ever been legally executed by the State of Texas, and that happened during the Civil War.[194]

In the end, neither would be executed or even serve much time behind bars. Two years into their sentence, a New Orleans appeals court ruled that Judge

Leslie Ashley and Carolyn Lima with their attorneys at the defense table. *From the Houston Metropolitan Research Center, Houston Public Library.*

Love had barred too much defense testimony. The court ordered new trials. At hers, Lima claimed that Leslie lead her into the whole ordeal, and a jury gave her five years. One April day in 1965, Lima walked out of Huntsville's Goree Unit a free woman. Declaring her love for hamburgers and bubble baths, her disdain for Leslie and her intentions to spend the rest of her life fixing hair and tending gardens, Carolyn Lima disappeared from the public eye.[195] Except for one thing: a 1966 adults-only biopic entitled *Burn, Baby, Burn: The Carolyn Lima Story.* "If They Didn't Pay for Play, She'd Burn Them Alive!" was the tagline; Lima was credited as a technical adviser.[196]

Leslie tried a new tack at his retrial: an insanity defense. It worked, and he was sent to a minimum-security mental institution, from which he quickly absconded and went on the lam, spending weeks as "Bobo the Clown" in a traveling carnival. Despite his presence on the FBI's Ten Most Wanted list, Leslie would elude capture for six months. His next trial, in Gatesville, wouldn't go as well as the last one: this time he was ruled sound of mind and sentenced to fifteen years on a prison farm.[197]

He served five years, chopping cotton in the Texas sun. Upon his release, his mother, Sylvia Ayres, at last fulfilled his fondest, longest-held wish: she paid for his sex-change operation. "Chop it off and throw it in the bayou!" he told a surgeon at Galveston's John Sealy Hospital. Leslie Douglas Ashley

Sylvia Ayres, Leslie Douglas Ashley's mother, outside the Harris County Courthouse. *From the Houston Metropolitan Research Center, Houston Public Library.*

renamed herself Leslie Elaine Green, an alias she had used on the lam, before changing it to Leslie Elaine Perez in honor of her prison lover.

Leslie returned to Houston and opened yet another bizarre chapter to her life. She went into local politics.

"Killer Transsexual in Runoff for County Chair," thundered the *Houston Chronicle* on the front page on March 14, 1991, ranking among the top ten headlines that paper has ever produced. "Give Leslie the Chair" was her motto. Her opponent was Ken Bentsen, nephew of the former vice presidential candidate Lloyd Bentsen. Bentsen explained away Leslie's strong showing by claiming that it reflected Hispanics pulling the lever for one they believed was of their own, and Bentsen easily won the runoff. Next up, Leslie sought a seat on city council, but she was barred from doing so by that pesky murder conviction. In 1999, her mother ran as her proxy against a popular and formidable young politico by the name of Annise Parker, whose destiny was to become the first openly gay mayor of a large American city. Parker crushed Ayres, who along with her son-turned-daughter became very enthusiastic AIDS activists. According to Bentley's *Dangerous Games*, at one point in the 1990s, Leslie was a regular at a Whataburger on South Main Street near the Astrodome. Her whereabouts since then are unknown.[198]

8
BEAVER CLEAVER'S AMERICA

Talk about Texas and cold war paranoia and murder, and most folks' minds alight on Dallas, the rabidly right-wing "City of Hate" where JFK met his doom. Houston's anti-communist hysteria and nuclear-doomsday dread might not have reached the stratospheric levels of its northern neighbor city, but there was enough conspiratorial weirdness, A-bomb terror, redbaiting and genuine fear and madness to go around. Indeed, the Museum District–Montrose area alone was either the scene of, tied to or the breeding ground of some of the most notorious crimes in Houston and even world history.

Tuesday, September 15, 1959, began like any other in Beaver Cleaver's America. Dozens of well-scrubbed boys in cuffed blue jeans and girls in long, puffy dresses converged on the tony, live oak–lined grounds of Edgar Allan Poe Elementary School. It was a sunny morning at the school just north of Rice Institute, and like so many sunny mornings in that halcyon era, students walked to school unchaperoned or pedaled there on Schwinns that they didn't bother to lock.[199]

Some kids likely debated the results of the season's first college football poll. Unveiled the day before, it was topped by the LSU Tigers, who, led by future Heisman Trophy winner Billy Cannon, would trounce the Owls from nearby Rice four days later. In celebrity news, Bing Crosby and his wife, after having five boys, finally had a girl, Mary, who would grow up to become an actress and eventually shoot J.R. Ewing on TV. *Bonanza*, the first network drama in living color, had premiered the Friday before.

A steady stream of gloriously finned and handsomely grilled Lincolns, Pontiacs and Cadillacs rumbled to the curbs of Hazard Street and gracious North and South Boulevards, their radios oozing musical caramel on the order of "Sleep Walk," "Sea of Love" and the latest Gentleman Jim Reeves hit or maybe crackling with reports of Khrushchev's first meeting with President Eisenhower on American soil. The portly premier had come to gloat; the day before, the Russian space agency had crash-landed an unmanned rocket on the moon.

Among the children walking to school that morning was Larry Schacht, a handsome, wavy-haired fifth-grader at the time, one of three children of Mona and Ezra Schacht, literally card-carrying members of the Communist Party and occasional targets for Ku Klux Klan integration.[200]

And *he* drove up too, in an ivory-and-green 1958 Chevy station wagon— tousle-headed Paul Harold Orgeron, along with his seven-year-old son, Dusty. Very much out of his element in the well-to-do neighborhood, the elder Orgeron had it in his head that he was going to enroll his tow-headed, freckle-faced son in Poe that morning, come hell or high water. Time was of the essence, he said; the term had already been underway for a week.[201]

The bell rang, and announcements began. Poe's principal, Ruth Doty, then in her fortieth year of working in Houston schools, got on the loudspeaker to lead the children through the Pledge of Allegiance before reciting her famously sing-song, falsetto renditions of the Lord's Prayer and the twenty-third Psalm: "Yea, though I walk through the valley of the shadow of death, I will fear no evil: for thou art with me."

At that moment, in Jennie Kolter's second-grade classroom, the students donned pairs of imaginary gloves, each holding up ten little fingers as they recited the ten words of the Golden Rule: "Do! Unto! Others! As! You! Would! Have! Done! Unto! You!"[202]

Meanwhile, in Principal Doty's office, Orgeron's attempt to enroll Dusty had run into a few snags. The recently divorced, unemployed tile-setter had been gently rebuffed by Doty's secretary, Juanita Weidner, after Orgeron could not produce any of Dusty's paperwork. Indeed, when asked, he could not even state his address, for he and Dusty had only been at the place—in what is today known as Midtown—for a couple of days.[203]

Appearing only slightly agitated, Orgeron promised to come back and straighten it all out the next day. But he returned just minutes later, and Orgeron's method of ending the impasse was something no one could have envisioned. A little over an hour later, on the playground at the rear of Poe, a suitcase-toting Orgeron and his son approached second-grade teacher

Patricia Johnston. "Teacher, read these," said Orgeron, handing Johnston two notes.

Johnston had trouble deciphering the chicken scratch that Orgeron, himself a second-grade dropout, handed her. Meanwhile, he mumbled about "the will of God" and "power in a suitcase." Looking down at the case, Johnston made a chilling discovery: there was a doorbell-type button affixed to the bottom of it. She became even more alarmed when Orgeron began insisting that she gather all her students around him. Johnston instead asked two students to fetch Principal Doty and school custodian James Montgomery and ordered the rest of the kids to go inside.[204]

Another teacher, Julia Whatley, had also become aware of the commotion and gone outside. According to police accounts, once Kolter arrived at the scene, Johnston handed her Orgeron's letters, even as the man kept talking about his suitcase full of power and how he "needed to get to the children." When Principal Doty and Montgomery arrived, Whatley and Johnston now, according to Johnston, fearing that Orgeron had something "horribly obscene" in his suitcase, hurriedly whisked more of the children inside.

Doty told Orgeron to leave the campus at once. Orgeron pointedly ignored her. "I have to follow the children to the second grade," he reportedly said, waving around the suitcase, which was later estimated to have contained something horribly obscene indeed: six sticks of dynamite primed to explode at the switch of an external trigger.

Nobody is certain what happened next. Montgomery, the custodian, may or may not have tussled with Orgeron, preventing him from entering the school with the suitcase (a blessing if true, because otherwise the ensuing explosion would have been even more catastrophic).

At that moment, two second graders, John Fitch Jr. and William Hawes Jr., were on their way to recess. Excited by the chance at some free time, they bolted ahead of their classmates and raced toward the playground.

Then came an eardrum-shredding boom. It was so loud it could be heard for blocks. The playground erupted in fire and flame. John Fitch and William Hawes ran straight into the blast and were killed, as were Montgomery, both Orgerons and Kolter. The blast stripped off every bit of Doty's clothing and broke her leg, but miraculously, she survived. Among the nineteen people taken to Hermann Hospital were two boys—Robert Taylor and Earl Fogler—each of whom had to have a mangled leg amputated.[205]

According to a *Time* magazine report a few days later, one of the boys was heard to sob, "That mean old man! That mean old man! Will somebody

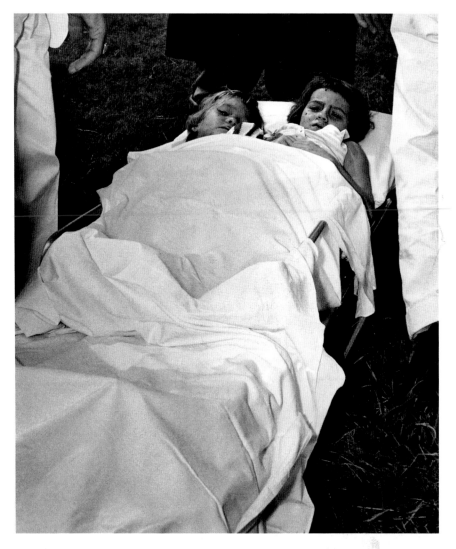

Two injured Poe students on a gurney. *From the Houston Metropolitan Research Center, Houston Public Library.*

get him? Will I need a crutch for my foot?" Then the seven-year-old asked a question for the ages: "Why did he have to do it?"

Years later, while still a guitar-strumming, Dylanesque high school golden boy, before his descent into drug addiction and ensuing recovery and final descent into one of modern humanity's ultimate madnesses, Larry Schacht would tell a high school girlfriend that he believed at the time that the blast had been a Soviet nuclear warhead detonating at or near Poe School. It was, after all, the fear that had been driven home to every American, even the son of Communist Party members.[206]

Survivor Bill Thomas thought the same thing. He remembers his teacher telling the kids to "duck and cover" under their desks. Even with his ears still ringing from the blast and classmates covered in shards of glass from imploded schoolroom windows, Thomas heard what he now believes were

HPD detectives examine bodies on the Poe School grounds. *From the Mike Vance collection.*

screams coming from the playground. At the time, however, he thought they were "bombs whistling down on us from all around," a legacy of a childhood steeped in nuclear paranoia and war movies.[207]

Then, to Schacht's and Thomas's relief, the fire-drill bell rang. (There was a different bell to signal nuclear Armageddon.) Schacht and Thomas and their schoolmates were marched out to the playground, as per protocol, but the protocol did not account for the scene of horror that greeted them there.

"We walked right into the massacre," says Thomas. "Even at that age, I was thinking, 'I don't think they meant to do this,' just sending us right out there. There were bodies out there, unidentifiable hunks of flesh, big gobs of...*something*."[208]

Soon, the schoolyard was bedlam—police and fire teams, gawkers, frantic parents, screaming and injured kids. Thomas recalls that one mother was in such a hysterical state that she ran right past her uninjured child.[209]

There were no grief counselors at the ready in 1959, no one to help the children process or reframe the experience. In fact, 1959 seemed to have

A quiet Poe classroom the day after the bombing. The date has not yet been changed on the blackboard. *From the Houston Metropolitan Research Center, Houston Public Library.*

only one piece of advice to offer those who witnessed the unimaginably awful: ignore it.

"We were marched right back to school the next day," one survivor recalled. Mrs. Kolter had been her teacher. "We had a substitute teacher, and we just went back."[210]

Many, perhaps most, did ignore it. Larry Schacht most decidedly did not, at least not in his mind.

Three years later, John F. Kennedy came to town to celebrate the groundbreaking of the Johnson Space Center and gave a memorable speech at Rice Stadium heralding the advent of the Apollo Program. He returned the following year on November 21, 1963, the last full day of his life.

Whether or not Larry Schacht was traumatized by the end of Camelot is unknown. What is known is that his parents were at least cursorily investigated in the aftermath. In December 1963, the Secret Service issued a memo about Ezra and Mona Schacht, describing Larry's mother as "an official in the State communist party and considered the top ranking communist in the Houston area."[211]

Some believe a far likelier suspect—a man who would achieve infamy for one of the grisliest double murders in Houston history—was living less than two miles away.

THE ICEBOX

At first, it seemed like a routine call to Houston cops C.M. Bullock and T.K. Bartha. On June 23, 1965, a nephew of the elderly Fred C. and Edwina Rogers had asked the police to check on the couple, as they hadn't been answering the phone for a few days.

The policemen forced their way into the locked house at 1815 Driscoll Street in Montrose—1.6 miles due north of Poe and a twenty-five-minute walk from the Schacht home on West Main Street—and found nothing amiss. At first. Bullock did think it was odd that food had been left on the dining room table, so on a whim, he decided to open the refrigerator. Still, nothing looked off.

Sure, there did seem to be an inordinate amount of meat in there, but hey, this is Texas. Bartha said that it looked like someone had slaughtered a hog. And then, just as Bullock was closing the door, something caught his eye: the severed heads of Mr. and Mrs. Rogers peeping out at him from the vegetable bins.

The Rogers home on Driscoll Street after their dismembered bodies were found. *From the Houston Metropolitan Research Center, Houston Public Library.*

Or perhaps "peeping" is not the right word, at least not in the case of Fred Rogers, as his eyes had been gouged out. He had first been beaten to death with a hammer; his wife had taken a single bullet to the head. Both had been dismembered in a bathroom, and their heads, legs and torsos were neatly stacked in the fridge. Some of their innards and sex organs were later found in a nearby sewer line, while the rest of their remains were never discovered.

A blood trail led to the bedroom of their reclusive forty-three-year-old son, Charles Frederick "Chuck" Rogers, a veteran of Naval Intelligence (cryptologist), commercial pilot and UH-educated seismologist who had mysteriously and suddenly quit his job several years before. Rogers was also a pilot and member of the Civil Air Patrol, a sort of flying National Guard, and it was in that service that he met one David Ferrie, a New Orleanian pilot with a reputation as a "chickenhawk" who preyed on young boys. Ferrie and Lee Harvey Oswald served in the same unit of the CAP in the late 1950s, a fact that would one day loom large in Orleans Parish district attorney Jim Garrison's investigation of Ferrie's alleged involvement in the JFK assassination.[212]

Crescent City private investigator Jack Martin also claimed that Ferrie had driven from New Orleans to Texas on the night of the assassination. Ferrie's story was that he and two friends drove 350 miles to the Winterland

Skating Rink in Houston, about 240 miles from Dallas, but a bare mile or so from the Rogers home, that evening. Ferrie said that "he had been considering for some time the feasibility and possibility of opening an ice-skating rink in New Orleans" and wanted to gather information on the ice rink business. "He stated that he introduced himself to [rink manager] Chuck Rolland and spoke with him at length concerning the cost of installation and operation of the rink." However, Rolland said that he never spoke to Ferrie about running an ice rink. Rolland said that Ferrie had spent his time at the rink's pay phone, making and receiving calls.[213]

Was Rogers somehow involved? Why was Ferrie in his old flyboy buddy's neighborhood on the day of the assassination? And what was Rogers up to?

Neighbors later said that they had not known that Rogers had lived there at all, as he was in the habit of rising before dawn and coming home after dark, even though he had no apparent job. Equally puzzling was the fact that Rogers was able to maintain and fly his own small airplane in and out of Hull Airport while having no visible means of support. It was also said that his only communication with his parents came in the form of notes shoved under the door of his attic bedroom.

This is only where it begins to get weird: some, most notably John R. Craig and A. Phillip Rogers (no relation), authors of *The Man on the Grassy Knoll*, later claimed that Rogers was a hit man for the Central Intelligence Agency (CIA). And not just any hit man but, along with Woody Harrelson's dad, Charles, one of two grassy knoll gunmen of JFK assassination lore. Rogers is also alleged to have posed as Lee Harvey Oswald on the assassin's sojourn in Mexico City.[214]

Local forensic artist Lois Gibson maintains that Rogers was one of the "three tramps" mysteriously arrested and released by Dallas police after the killing of the president.

This theory posits that Rogers' parents found his notebooks and had been tracking his phone calls. Having learned too much, Rogers rubbed them out and disappeared.[215]

Yes, it's far-fetched. Why the CIA would house a key operative in his parents' attic bedroom and why that master spy would make the amateurish mistake of allowing one of his top-secret diaries to fall into the hands of hostile parental units remain a mystery. Not to mention the sane presumption that CIA-sanctioned hits don't need to involve mutilation and dismemberment.

Still, some versions of this story also maintain that Rogers was also

"Raoul" or "Frenchy," James Earl Ray's handler in the assassination of Martin Luther King Jr. James Ellroy has found him compelling enough to make him a character in both *American Tabloid* and *The Cold Six Thousand*.

All that speculation and intrigue was to come. All the police knew in summer 1965 was that an elderly couple had been savagely hacked to pieces, and their odd son was nowhere to be found.

Police also found a bloodstained saw in his room, but as for Rogers himself, the trail ended there. Some said he snuck off to Canada, while others insisted he was living off the land in the Big Thicket, the East Texas wilds he frequently visited alone for weeks at a stretch. One Houston cop claimed he put his pilot's license to good use in his new home of Alaska.[216]

With regard to the murders of his parents, police sought Rogers as a material witness in what became known as the "Icebox Murders" but had given up by 1975, when he was declared dead by a local judge. And to think it all started with a routine welfare-of-the-elderly check gone wrong on Driscoll Street.

LARRY SCHACHT FINDS HIS CONFIDENCE

The Icebox Murders occurred the same year that Sherrie Tatum met Larry Schacht, who would become one of her high school boyfriends. She recalled a boy incensed at his elders for their seeming lack of compassion in the aftermath of the bombing. After all, the kids already suffered from generalized A-bomb angst, he would rail in their hours-long, puppy-love phone calls. *Didn't they understand that?* "He still had that sense of outrage," Tatum said. "This affected him so deeply."[217]

She recalls that Schacht was doing pretty well at seventeen. Slim, dark, intense and handsome, he was a bit of a junior rock star. They first met at a Tuesday after-school folksinging club at Bellaire High School, where Tatum attended. Larry was then a student at Lamar and came by with a friend.

"We would usually sing Kingston Trio songs in unison, and here comes Larry, and he looked all bad-boy. He just walked in there, sat on Miss Donovan's desk, played his guitar and sang *solo*. So that was quite electrifying. We were like, 'Who *is* this guy? He doesn't even go to our school. Who does he think he *is*?' And then he asked for a cigarette! On school property!"[218]

Tatum obliged the suave and solemn songster. Then she ran into Larry again a little later, this time at an anti-Vietnam rally, where Sherrie and Larry smoked pot and struck up a romance that later receded into a friendship with romantic overtones. Sherrie would feel awkward introducing her new boyfriends to Larry; Larry would often express his disapproval of them, telling her they weren't sensitive enough for her. In other words, they weren't like Larry, who painted and played Dylan songs on the guitar.[219]

"Everything always felt like a test with Larry," Sherrie says. "He was like one of those diamond merchants from Amsterdam. Always *examining.*"[220]

Larry was also on the receiving end of examinations,

Larry Schacht's photo from the 1966 *Orenda* yearbook at Lamar High School. *From the Houston Metropolitan Research Center, Houston Public Library.*

both official and paramilitary. The FBI was keenly aware of his parents' radical activities, and Larry himself is rumored to have founded a Lamar High School chapter of the radical youth group Students for a Democratic Society. It's an established fact that his brother Danny did the same thing at the University of Houston, and he was eventually prosecuted for his antiwar activities. FBI memos that would surface in 1978 confirmed that the G-Men knew young Larry—then a high school junior—enjoyed marijuana and LSD.[221]

It wasn't just the FBI; the Klan is reported to have left a flaming cross on the Schachts' front yard. For southern rednecks, as Jewish Yankee communists, the Schachts epitomized "outside agitators," even if they had been in Houston for years.

All of this surveillance and intimidation fed young Larry's paranoid worldview. And you know what they say—you aren't paranoid if they really are out to get you.

Over the next few years, Larry and Sherrie would run into each other at parties, and it soon became apparent that Larry had gone beyond the usual hippie drugs like pot and acid and had taken to shooting up meth. "Living in Houston, where everything is so slow and sticky, kinda drove him crazy," Sherrie says. "I think he needed that for stimulation."[222]

Larry soon became addicted. Sherrie says he seemed like a hopeless case. Toward the end, it became apparent that the once-promising Larry was bound for prison, the nuthouse or an early grave. Sherrie saw Larry in Austin in May 1970. He told her he was heading out to California. That was the last time Sherrie saw him.[223]

"I have always considered it a miracle that I left Texas," Schacht wrote years later, in 1977. "I had done five years in the drug scene, and after 150 trips on psychedelic drugs and two years shooting speed, I was wasted."[224]

Schacht reportedly had twin visions, one that instructed him to go to California and another that led him to a healer of sorts, one who saw potential in the strung-out Texan and weaned him off the meth. This man introduced Larry to the Christian God—a version keenly interested in radical politics and justice for the poor—and helped him pay his way all through medical school. Larry found that shaman seventy-two hours after his arrival in the Golden State.[225]

"I have always considered it a miracle that I left Texas, traveled to California, and heard Jim Jones speak my third day in that new state," he would later state in an affidavit, a year before his demise alongside Jones.[226]

The good reverend likely saw Schacht's first appearance at one of his services as equally miraculous. After all, as an anonymous People's Temple adherent would later tell the FBI, Schacht was less made of human clay for Jones to mold than he was molten gold: "Schacht was quickly evaluated by Reverend Jones and members of [the] 'inner circle' as [an] extremely intelligent individual who demonstrated unstable, insecure emotional state. Schacht possessed dissatisfaction with 'state of things in general.' Schacht characterized as extremely rebellious personality...It was these personality flaws which prompted Jones to personally select Schacht to attend medical to serve Jones' and PT ends."[227]

In short, Schacht was the sort for Jones' inner sanctum: a brilliant "loner" who could be "used as [a] tool by Jones."[228]

According to later investigators, before he started paying young Larry's way through medical school, Jones wanted first to achieve physical communion with his confused young protégé. "Jim Jones has always shown great love and concern for me. He permitted me to accept my bisexual nature by having sexual relations with me at my request before I went to medical school. He penetrated me in the anus." This in turn gave Schacht the confidence he needed to become a doctor and "fulfill my goal to be of service to suffering humanity in the medical profession." Or so they say Schacht said.[229]

A few years later, with degree in hand and a San Francisco–area internship under his belt, Schacht told his friends that he and Jones were heading down to South America, where he—by now Dr. Laurence Schacht—would serve as a medical missionary for the People's Temple. As that utopia collapsed under the weight of Jones' drug-induced delusions and paranoia into a totalitarian, Marxist jungle hellhole, Jones tasked his ever-loyal medicine man with finding the best way to efficiently and quickly dispatch every one of the nine-hundred-plus members of the People's Temple, while not unleashing panic among those who had second thoughts or never wished to die to begin with.[230]

Schacht attacked the problem of mass "revolutionary suicide" in the same methodical, questioning manner that Tatum likened to a diamond cutter. He considered and rejected germicidal means. "Botulism + staphylocci [*sic*] in process now," he wrote in a letter to Jones in January 1978.[231]

He also assured his mentor that his bedside manner was up to the enormity of the task. "I am quite capable of organizing the suicide aspect + will follow through + try to convey concern + warmth throughout the ordeal," he wrote to Jones.

After poring over books and medical journals for almost a year, Schacht at last concluded that cyanide was their best bet.

"I had some misgivings about its effectiveness, but from further research I have gained more confidence in it, at least theoretically," he confided to Jones in an undated memo. "I would like to give about two grams to a large pig to see how effective our batch is to be sure we don't get stuck with a disaster like would occur if we used thousands of pills to sedate the people and then the cyanide was not good enough to do the job."[232]

And so, along with Valium, chloral hydrate and Phenergan, that was what Schacht mixed with grape Flavor Aid and administered to more than nine hundred people. And it's almost certain that Schacht was set on that path on that terrible September day at Edgar Allan Poe Elementary School.[233]

STACY AND BUNNI

S ex Pistol Sid Vicious' alleged murder of Nancy Spungen has entered rock-and-roll lore through the film *Sid and Nancy*, a gritty portrayal of the last of the drug-addled British punk rocker and his American lover, both strung out on heroin and dwelling in domestic disharmony in New York's Chelsea Hotel. That was where Vicious allegedly stabbed Spungen to death, but the twenty-one-year-old died of a heroin overdose before his case came to trial.

A murder in Houston's Montrose district six months prior was uncannily similar. Two lovers united by chemicals; a musician whose band changed the course of rock history but who was then in the doldrums of career apathy, burnout and addiction. A homicide and no conviction.

Some bands are just fated to live fast, die hard and leave a pretty corpse. Maybe no Texas group ever exemplified that credo better than the 13th Floor Elevators, perhaps the first and certainly one of the most dramatic exemplars of a band that flew too close to the sun.

Along with singer and guitarist Roky Erickson and lyricist and electric jug player Tommy Hall, guitarist Stacy Keith Sutherland was a founding member and a mainstay in the ever-evolving cast of 13th Floor Elevators. Hall decreed early on that the band should never pick up an instrument—whether rehearsing or performing publicly—without first dosing heavily on LSD, and let's just say that the Elevators picked up their instruments pretty often.[234]

Nobody knew then what dangers lurked in long-term use of LSD, so the Elevators found out the hard way that what Hall called their "quest for pure sanity" was a dangerous trip. Sutherland once recalled trying to perform while lit up by a very heavy dose. He recalled that the audience started to glow and then turned first into wolves and then into angels who had the power to determine if Sutherland would be allowed to live or condemned to die.

This was the kind of spiritual ordeal the Elevators taxed themselves with night after night—Sutherland once recalled that the members dropped acid a few times a week every week for five straight years, even though the majority of their trips were bad ones, in his recollection. The astral qualities of getting high infused their lyrics, and Hall even alluded to their drug devotion to Dick Clark on *American Bandstand* in 1966. It was all in an effort to create music that came from, as Roky Erickson put it, "where the pyramid meets the eye."[235]

Like Janis Joplin, the Elevators headed from Houston and Austin to San Francisco and became mainstays of the Bay Area music and counterculture scene before returning to Texas in 1967. They headlined the Fillmore and the Avalon, the meccas that hosted most every major band of the era. Their live shows were known by many to be "truly a thing of legend."[236]

They lasted intact for two signature albums and a few lesser vinyl efforts before imploding for good at the end of the '60s, beset from within by their own overstretched souls and from without by the long arm of the law. By the early '70s, half the former band members were hooked on meth, and Erickson slipped over into a string of drug busts and incarcerations and into the grips of an insanity from which he would not escape until early in the 2000s, when his younger brother, Sumner Erickson, took control of his affairs. Hall migrated back to San Francisco, where he has spent the last few decades in a Tenderloin fleapit hotel, regularly ingesting psychedelic drugs and unraveling the secrets of the universe.[237]

While they were not chart-topping hit makers while active, the band's music developed a cult-like following decades after they broke up. Today, they are credited with either being the first or among the first psychedelic rock bands. Their biggest hit, "You're Gonna Miss Me," is the centerpiece of the opening scene of *High Fidelity*, that cinematic ode to rock-and-roll critical snobbery. Bands as diverse as REM, Queens of the Stone Age and Okkervil River have declared them a major influence. They were even the subject of a 2005 documentary.[238]

After a short stint in prison for his own drug busts, Stacy Sutherland, a native of Kerrville in the Hill Country, returned to Houston, where International Artists, his band's record label, was headquartered and where they had lived for a time on a ramshackle estate off Old Galveston Road known as "the Funky Mansions." Sutherland was primarily drawn to Houston by an old girlfriend named Anne Elizabeth Bunnell, a vivacious, dishwater blonde with two kids and a MENSA-level IQ but the life skills of a child.

"She couldn't handle the everyday little things in life," former neighbor Jim Hord told blogger Ivan "Koop" Kuper in 2011. "Bunni displayed bad judgment in men and had a lot of slime-ball friends."[239]

She divided her time between drinking and drugging, dancing at a notorious Montrose strip club called Boobie Rock and aspiring to become a court reporter. Patrons at the Boobie Rock called her "Bunni," and the name stuck.

By then, Sutherland was no longer gobbling huge amounts of LSD, mescaline and magic mushrooms every week, which is not to say his appetite for narcotics had been sated. Like many veterans of the Summer of Love, he had turned from psychedelics to heroin, cocaine and amphetamines. Basically, Sutherland would try whatever came his way, according to friend Hord, and by the mid-'70s, his addictions to both drink and drugs had elbowed aside all his musical aspirations.[240]

"I don't remember ever hearing Stacy play guitar when I went over to visit. He used to talk about drugs a lot. He had a fascination with drugs, and he would do anything that came his way," Hord told Kuper. "Bunni once told me that when she and Stacy used to go out bar hopping in the neighborhood, Stacy would bandage his hand before leaving the house, and when people would buy him drinks and ask him to play guitar with the band, he would have an excuse not to play and sit in with them, choosing to drink all night instead."[241]

Stacy and Bunni were wed in 1976, on Stacy's thirty-first birthday, and settled into a home at 516 Pacific Street, in what is now the epicenter of Houston's hard-partying gay district. Hord told Kuper that their domestic situation was not one likely to crack the covers of *Better Homes and Gardens*, to put it mildly. Nor were their domestic relations of the *Little House on the Prairie* variety.

"Stacy had a very bad temper, and the alcohol brought out the worst in him," said Hord. "But Stacy and Bunni brought out the worst in each other. The house was always dirty, and it was infested with roaches. Bunni wasn't the best housekeeper. Every time I went over to visit, the condition of the house used to really bug me. Bunni had some really bad times in her life, but the time spent with Stacy was the worst."[242]

In the wee hours of August 24, 1978, roughly fourteen months after their wedding day, Bunni ended a full day of drunken quarreling by shooting Stacy in the stomach with a .22-caliber rifle in the kitchen of the Pacific Street bungalow at about 3:30 a.m.[243]

At 5:07 a.m., Sutherland was pronounced dead at Ben Taub hospital. Rumor has it that shortly after the murder, Bunni took Sutherland's bloodstained guitar to mutual friend Frank Davis, the studio engineer on some of the Elevators' finest work. "Stacy would have wanted you to have this," Bunni reportedly told an aghast Davis.[244]

Hord believed that Sutherland had gotten belligerent with Bunni's fifteen-year-old son. "And when Stacy lunged at Bunni in an attempt to enter her son's bedroom, she pulled the trigger to the .22 rife that the couple kept in the house for protection against burglars."

Prosecutors brought a murder case against Bunni, and the grand jury indicted her, but two years later, the case was dismissed under a law that was on the books then called the "Speedy Trial Act of 1974." The judge thought the defendant had waited long enough. Bunni finally did become a court reporter, remarried and stayed in the Pacific Street house until her death from cancer at age forty-three in 1987.[245]

Stacy Sutherland was buried in a Kerrville cemetery, back near where he had practiced guitar near the Guadalupe River. It is doubtful that many in what was then a conservative Hill Country town understood much of his rise or fall. The local newspaper's coverage of his murder consisted of just one run-on sentence: "We are sorry to learn of the death of Stacy Sutherland, the family has our sympathy."[246]

10
TWO CANDY MEN

Houston, and Houston alone, has the dubious distinction of having not one but two "Candy Man" killers. Dean Corll was the most prolific; indeed, he and accomplices David Owen Brooks and Elmer Wayne Henley are among the most savage and prolific in world history, claiming a minimum of twenty-eight young male victims between 1970 and 1973, when Henley murdered Corll at the behest of a would-be victim. Years later, Chicago's killer clown, John Wayne Gacy, would say that Corll—like Gacy a sadist and a deeply repressed homosexual—had been an inspiration on his way to surpassing what was then the record for victims in a serial murder case.

The full saga of Corll, Henley and Brooks is recounted in multiple books and a movie. It was a story that stunned the nation; they had never seen an intimate evil on that scale before. And not surprisingly, it held a vise grip on Houstonians, who watched the latest discoveries of bodies on their black-and-white TVs each evening. To this day, many longtime residents of the Heights recall schoolmates who were Corll victims—either bodies found or kids written off as runaways who were never heard from again.

In August 1973, after Elmer Wayne Henley pumped five slugs into Corll's chest and then called home to say, "Mama, I killed Dean," unleashing the cascading stories of horror, the local and national press ran a litany of articles that could almost be used as a template for modern media coverage of mass murderers.

Law enforcement officers search for Corll, Henley and Brooks victims as beachgoers and reporters look on. *From the Houston Metropolitan Research Center, Houston Public Library.*

Dean Corll was an unremarkable student and a trombone player in the band at Vidor High School, east of Beaumont. His band teacher had to be shown a yearbook photo before he even recalled the guy. Friends and relatives in Vidor knew him to be quiet, polite and clean cut, "a good boy" who liked girls. He moved to Houston in 1962 and worked in the family business. A couple of years later, Corll served a ten-month stint in the army, getting an honorable discharge as a hardship case. His mother had no doubt that he was innocent and that his name would be cleared.[247]

"Let me put it this way," his best pal from high school told the Associated Press. "If Dean Corll had knocked on my door before last Wednesday when the story broke, I would have invited him in for a beer."[248]

Only a few mothers claimed to have an uneasy feeling about the man who offered sweets to neighborhood children. There was seemingly no hint that he was "the Fagan of a homosexual rape and mass murder ring." In short, nobody knew much of anything before the pictures of torture boards, recruited murder accomplices and a boat shed full of bodies invaded their dinnertime, and after that, there were plenty of sleepless nights.[249]

Corll was called the "Candy Man" because he operated a candy company. Ronald Clark O'Bryan was known as such because candy was his murder weapon. While O'Bryan only claimed a single victim, his crime might have had even more far-reaching implications than Corll's. After all, it's not for nothing that O'Bryan came to be known nationwide as the "Man Who Killed Halloween."

A pall hung over Pasadena's Second Baptist Church on that November Sunday in 1974. The bereaving flock had just lost one of their littlest lambs—eight-year-old Timothy O'Bryan—and his demise had been horrible indeed. Some demented soul had handed the boy a Pixy Stix candy laced with potassium cyanide on Halloween night, and after eating it just before bedtime, the boy died, vomiting uncontrollably, his tiny body wracked with convulsions and, finally, frothing at the mouth. He was dead within an hour of his arrival at an area hospital.

The senseless death of little Tim shrouded the congregation. What monster dwelled in Pasadena, brutally killing children for no reason at all? How could such evil visit the family of such a wonderful man as Timothy's father, Ronald Clark O'Bryan?

And then the elder O'Bryan, a dedicated parishioner and chorister, rose and took a solo turn on the classic hymn "Blessed Assurance," paraphrasing the refrain somewhat:

"This is Tim's stor-eee, this is Tim's song," the big, bespectacled, sandy-haired man sang in his oddly high, crystalline tenor. "Praising my sav-ioorrrr, all the day looonng..."

"There wasn't a dry eye in the church when he was through," a member of the congregation would later say. "He had the entire church in a very emotional state, that this man was so strong in his faith and his convictions that he could do this."

At the time, none of the elder O'Bryan's fellow believers had an inkling just *what* he was capable of. "I've seen a person or two who more closely fit the stereotype of the dangerous sociopath," says former Harris County assistant district attorney Victor Driscoll, who helped Mike Hinton prosecute the case. "But no one who had that appearance of being a trusted part of the community or neighborhood, who had that mask, that ability to calculate and do what he did."[250]

But in the weeks to come, hardened crime reporters in Houston would note that while the thirty-year-old O'Bryan had been quite right to alter the words to his hymn of choice, he should have gone ahead and changed the title to "Blessed Insurance" while he was at it.

For it would soon emerge that it was none other than O'Bryan himself who, as Driscoll put it at his trial, "sacrificed his son on the altar of greed."[251]

In doing so, O'Bryan not only killed his own son but also (temporarily) ended Halloween for a generation of Houstonians. As one of his own attorneys would admit in open court, "As you know, my client is convicted of killing Halloween."

"It changed the way we did things and our anxieties about things on a much smaller scale than 9/11 changed the country itself," Driscoll says. "It caused a completely different focus on what we did, how we did it, what our sensibilities were, and it made us more wary of our neighbors and people that we knew."[252]

The year 1974 had been rough for the O'Bryan family. In fact, none of the years Ronald had been married to his wife, Daynene, had been particularly prosperous. By Daynene's count, Ronald had cycled through twenty-one jobs between 1969 and 1974, when he found yet another gig as an optometrist at Texas State Opticians.

And by early October, Ronald was eight months behind on his car note, facing a total of $100,000 in various debts and trying to support a family of four on $150 a week. He and Daynene had already moved to a smaller home in Deer Park, but the downsizing did little more than chip away at their mountain of woes.

In January 1974, O'Bryan took out $10,000 life insurance policies, one each on little Timothy and Timothy's five-year-old sister, Elizabeth. Because Daynene had objected to those purchases, Ronald kept the next ones close to his vest: in early October, he secretly took out additional $20,000 policies on each of the kids and paid the premiums in cash.[253]

At around the same time, O'Bryan had been asking his TSO co-workers and his friends about cyanide. Where could he get some, he wondered. Up until the 1950s, optometrists had used cyanide to clean gold frames, but that method had long since been replaced by safer ones. O'Bryan claimed that he was interested in trying out the old method.

But—just out of curiosity—how much would it take to kill a man, he asked. Again, just out of curiosity, how easy it was to detect in a corpse? A few days before Halloween, he visited a Houston chemical supplier and left disappointed when he was told he would have to buy at least five pounds of cyanide. Meanwhile, he told a creditor that he was expecting to come in for a large windfall soon—*very* soon.

"He was so calculating that it overrode any good judgment that may have existed," Driscoll says.[254]

O'Bryan was uncharacteristically excited as the holiday approached, springing for costumes for his kids and volunteering to accompany another dad, a man named Jim Bates, on his trick-or-treating rounds with the two Bates kids. The group set out into the cool and rainy Pasadena night, Ronald still clad in his white TSO lab coat.[255]

One of the homes was darkened, and after a perfunctory knock, Ronald lingered behind as the Bateses and the O'Bryan children moved on next door. He caught up with the group brandishing several jumbo-sized Pixy Stix, exulting that Bates must have had some "rich neighbors." Later that night, at the Bates home, O'Bryan distributed a Pixy Stix to each of the kids in the party and handed another to a boy named Whitney Parker, a trick-or-treater at Bates' door. And then O'Bryan took his kids back to Deer Park.[256]

As Halloween drew to a close, Daynene went out to call on a friend, leaving Ronald alone with the kids. Sugar-bleary Tim begged for one last treat before bed, and dad heartily recommended the huge Pixy Stix. The sugary powder had hardened near the top of the tube, so his father obligingly crushed the cyanide-laced candy and then poured it in his son's mouth. Tim complained that it was bitter, so Ronald washed it down with Kool-Aid. Tim was violently ill almost immediately and pronounced dead within hours.

The rapid action of the poison almost certainly saved O'Bryan's daughter, Elizabeth, and possibly the three other children, Driscoll believes. "Both of his children were going to ingest that," Driscoll says. Ronald Clark O'Bryan didn't buy all that insurance only to cash in half of it, after all. "But [Tim] went into convulsions so quickly, O'Bryan kinda got diverted from giving it to his other child. This is conjecture, but I think he thought that several children in random homes would wake up dead the next morning. It would be random, there would be others including his own, and there would be no connecting him to it. But he didn't realize how quickly it would react."[257]

Over at the hospital, doctors rapidly diagnosed cyanide poisoning and determined that the Pixy Stix was the vessel of doom. Pasadena police frantically searched for the other tainted treats all through the night. One was found unopened in a sleeping boy's hand, and another child had come seconds from death.[258]

Driscoll recalls that one of the Bates children started to tear open a Pixy Stix just before bedtime, but his mother told him it was "outside candy" and that he could eat it tomorrow. "It was just kind of an afterthought," Driscoll says. "Just sort of, 'No, no, no, let's not do that tonight.' It was just so close. That there weren't other deaths was just circumstance and chance. One touch of that cyanide to your tongue was almost instantly fatal." Indeed, each of the candies was found to contain enough poison to kill two or three adults.[259]

According to Daynene, back at the O'Bryan house, Ronald "beat the wall" and yelled "why an eight-year-old boy had to die." "I did not see any tears," she added.

Bright and early the very next morning, his son's body still in the morgue, Ronald was down at the insurance office, trying to collect that $30,000.[260]

Police wouldn't learn about O'Bryan's insurance policies for several days. After questioning the O'Bryans, they still sought a random madman. Over time, that scenario became less and less convincing.

"The police did several days of investigation and finally came to the conclusion that there just wasn't anybody else [other than O'Bryan]," Driscoll says. "The crime was confined to a certain neighborhood, a certain evening and a certain number of people. They kept getting loose ends, and O'Bryan had pointed out a house where he'd gotten the Pixy Stix, and it turned out those people weren't home on Halloween."[261]

Detectives amassed a mountain of evidence. They eventually assembled twelve people who said O'Bryan asked them about cyanide. There were those odd insurance purchases. The man in the dark home who O'Bryan claimed had given him the candy had been working at Hobby Airport until eleven o'clock on Halloween night and had two hundred witnesses supporting his alibi. They heard about O'Bryan's firm, inexplicable prediction that his finances were about to improve in a big way. Driscoll says investigators also found that O'Bryan had recently conducted two petty insurance frauds—one on his car and another on some clothes he claimed were destroyed by a washateria—in the months leading up to the murder. They also had reason to believe O'Bryan had been swindling Second Baptist Church.

"He was always positioning himself as being very important at his church," Driscoll says. "I think he was treasurer or something, and I believe he inflated his own contribution records and probably was embezzling some of the funds."[262]

They brought the O'Bryans back in and questioned them in separate rooms. Daynene was ruled out as a suspect. Her husband—not so much.

Driscoll recalls that O'Bryan was on the threshold of confessing but stopped just short. Even without a confession, police had enough

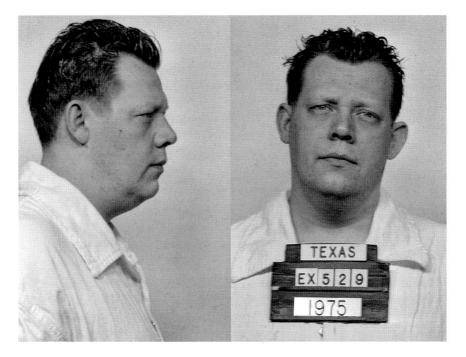

Ronald Clark O'Bryan's official mug shot for death row. *From the TDCJ Archives.*

evidence to make an arrest. His neighbors were shocked. They couldn't believe a Christian gentleman—a soloist in a Baptist church choir, a man whose only brush with the law had been a parking ticket or two—could be capable of such wickedness. "Until I hear his own statement that he did it, I'll never believe it," said one neighbor. "There has to be foul-up somewhere," said another. "I don't feel that he could do that at all."

One person who was less astonished: Daynene O'Bryan. "In the back of her mind she was afraid that would happen, but she was hoping that they would find another person that did it," Driscoll says. "She didn't want to think that Ronald did it, but she said it didn't come as a complete surprise to her."[263]

At his trial, the jury of ten men and two women didn't buy the choirboy act, either. The defense argued that all of the evidence was circumstantial, but to no avail. At one point, O'Bryan turned to prosecutor Hinton and offered him a Tootsie Roll. Hinton was not amused. O'Bryan's conviction came after forty-six minutes of deliberation.[264]

"The only inescapable conclusion is that this man killed his own flesh and blood for money," Hinton thundered in arguing for O'Bryan's execution. "Think how easy it would be for him to kill a stranger for money. We owe a debt to future innocent victims to carve this cancer from our society."[265] After seventy-one minutes of deliberation, the jury agreed.[266]

O'Bryan left his own child in a grave, and his actions also ruined Halloween for an entire generation of American kids. "It went to the core of our insecurity because this wasn't kids just running the neighborhood—they were with their parents in their own neighborhood in a group," Driscoll says. "It was about as secure a way as you can do it."[267]

Though it was only a decade earlier, Elmer Wayne Henley was not eligible for the death penalty in the other Candy Man murders. It was ruled unconstitutional in the United States at the time, and Henley instead faced six ninety-nine-year terms. Sensibilities were different for the other Candy Man. Only the most ardent death penalty opponents protested outside the Walls in Huntsville on March 31, 1984—O'Bryan's date with the needle.[268]

Instead, as O'Bryan, who maintained his innocence to the last, feasted on a last meal of well-done steak, sweet tea and Boston cream pie, a raucous, beery and vengeance-minded crowd of students from nearby

Sam Houston State—some in Halloween masks, one waving a giant replica of a Pixy Stix—chanted, "Trick-or-treat!"[269]

Across the state in Amarillo, prosecutor Mike Hinton floated on a raft in a lake and toasted the heavens with a bottle of beer. Driscoll could not manage even as feeble a celebration as that.

"The process worked to its end, and his execution was the end of that process, but it was just too tragic to celebrate any part of it, including his execution," he says.[270]

11
THE TODVILLE MURDER MANSION

In the fall of 1984, a mortified Houston watched as then-prosecutor Rusty Hardin tried accused murderer Danny Lee Garrett. That spring, Garrett's co-defendant, Karla Faye Tucker, had been convicted in a separate trial and sentenced to death for her role in the horrific pickaxe slayings of Jerry Lynn Dean and Deborah Thornton, and Garrett would soon join Tucker on death row.

Meanwhile, a few miles southwest of the courthouse, the tenderloin district near the corner of Westheimer and Montrose was teeming with young, male street hustlers, even more so than today. The rents are skyrocketing now, but back then, Montrose was still sliding downward as the oil bust extended into its third year. Cheap rents abounded. Thousands of kids ended up there, where many succumbed to selling their young bodies to aging sugar daddies in exchange for money, booze, crack, smack, crank, acid or X.

For such a big city, '80s Houston was, in some ways, still a small town. Case in point: the teenage ritual of cruising Westheimer Road, in which the fourth-largest city in America did its best to impersonate a one–Dairy Queen town, one where all you can do is drive down the strip and then turn back around. While cruising Westheimer has multiple connotations, especially as you approach Bagby, back in the Reagan era, to most it meant getting in your car and driving aimlessly east from west Houston, gawking at the freak show in the Montrose area and turning around on Elgin Street and heading back out.

This was oil-bust Houston, and it looked then like Montrose might become a full-on slum. There were no condos along 'Theimer (as it was often called by the mullet set) and few fancy restaurants. From Montrose Boulevard all the way to what is now called Midtown, Westheimer was lined with little more than one "modeling studio" after another, and it seems like there were even more tattoo shops than there are now. The denizens and visitors to these businesses (not to mention the street hustlers, drag queens, punks and Guardian Angels who still lurk in the area) provided plenty for the hordes of suburbanites—getting their first taste of freedom and big-city life—to gawk at from the safety of their Blazers and Cutlasses.

On weekend nights, Westheimer would be bumper-to-bumper from Bagby to well past Buffalo Speedway and sometimes all the way out to the Galleria, a phantasmagoria of teenage hormones and sound collisions: car horns, engines revving, squealing girls, the hiss and almost subsonic bass rumble of "Paul Revere" booming from a Jeep Cherokee interlocking with a Honda CRX chirping out that inane "Two of Hearts" pop ditty or the root canal Teutonic skronk of that "Warm Leatherette" monstrosity.

Though neither a runaway nor a prostitute, twenty-three-year-old Jeff Statton was in the thick of the Lower Westheimer scene. Statton had an auto theft conviction and a stay in a mental hospital under his belt. He was also shooting heroin and living with a seventeen-year-old kid named Lance, and with their eviction from their Montrose apartment looming, Lance said he knew an older guy who would take them in.[271]

This older guy was Bill List, a portly, balding, fifty-seven-year-old businessman. After a stint in the coffin-and-crypt trade and an early '60s prison stay (for sex with underage boys) and ensuing divorce, the Ohio native made a fortune in the '70s with a trailer rental business. While so many of his neighbors were scraping by, List was living large on Galveston Bay.[272]

There, on Seabrook's Todville Road, List built his dream home: a two-story, thirty-four-thousand-square-foot, brick, prison-looking leviathan with white wrought iron–encrusted verandas wrapping both floors. Inside, List had placed several huge bars, hundreds of potted plants, multiple Jacuzzis, an enormous game room and an atrium complete with indoor swimming pool. In the terrazzo-tiled lobby, List installed a sneeze-shielded steam table, the better to serve guests at his thirty-five-foot dinner table.[273]

"You didn't know whether to be impressed, amazed or disgusted," Statton recalled. "The sheer size was impressive, but then you'd look closer and it was, 'What kind of hideous thing is this monstrosity?'" Statton says that for much of his stay in the "Holiday Inn on acid," most of the rooms were unfurnished. One day, List dispatched a moving truck to the mansion. "I was all excited. I wanted to bring people over," Statton remembers. It turns out List had purchased a defunct hotel's inventory. "He had bought all these tweed couches and paintings that had magic marker prices written on the back of them. Just *craziness*. No sense to the whole thing."[274]

No sense, save for the logic of pure ostentation. List loved to exaggerate his importance and inflate his wealth, and the mansion was a tangible expression of his character. List was much less showy in his personal appearance. When Statton first arrived, he says, List came to the door shirtless and barefoot, wearing only a pair of checkered polyester pants. What little hair he had stood straight up from his head. (He refused to buy shampoo or shaving cream, as both were a waste of money. Bar soap sufficed for both shaving and hair washing.) Statton thought he was a caretaker.[275]

Estranged from his ex-wife and adult son and daughter, both of whom had changed their last names to distance themselves from their dad, List was free to spend the rest of his days indulging his passion: cruising Montrose for teenage boys. Once ensconced in his sprawling bayside lair, List would feed them, give them access to booze and look the other way if they did drugs. And a lavish-if-tacky roof was over their heads, so long as they agreed to help with the cooking, general upkeep...and other things.

Namely sex, and Bill List's appetites were reportedly even more hideous than his mansion, unprintable perversions that required a never-ending supply of fresh hustlers. While many were taken with the party lifestyle of the mansion at first, few could abide List's demands for long. "He used the power that his money brought over homeless, hopeless teenage boys," Statton says. "He'd promise them something, bring them *all* the way out to Seabrook with no ride back. And then he'd be like, 'Here's twenty bucks. If you don't like it, fuck you.'"[276]

On October 17, 1984, there were four young denizens of the mansion. Statton says it was a "bad combination of people." There was nineteen-year-old Elbert Ervin Holman, an angry, Pasadena-bred heroin user and crank addict, a dropout of the tenderloin's Covenant House teen shelter already convicted of stabbing and robbing a fellow teen. Ironically, he was known on the streets as "Smiley." Statton says he had warned List about kids like Smiley. "I'd tell him, 'These are not Saint John's kids you are messin' with. These are street kids. One of these days, one of them is gonna kill you.' And he'd be like, 'Aww, I ain't worried about them. I can take care of myself.'"[277]

There was also Smiley's running buddy, Tim Foran, aka "Peppermint," a nineteen-year-old dead-end kid from downstate Illinois. It was Peppermint who introduced Smiley to List in Montrose.

And there was "Joey," a sixteen-year-old runaway from Tomball List had pounced on when he found him shooting pool at the Midnight Sun bar on Westheimer. "I was involved with Joey, and Bill repeatedly coerced Joey into sexual deals," Statton says. Statton says List subjected Joey to a constant barrage of emotional blackmail, telling him that he had to have sex with him or he would kick him out. "And you know Jeff's not gonna go with you, because Jeff wants to stay here," List would say. "He's the only person you have, and you will lose him."[278]

Statton says a desperate Joey finally told him all that had been going on. Statton then confronted List and declared his feelings for Joey. "I told him we were in a serious relationship, well, at the time I *thought* it was a serious relationship, and that he would have to stop. He told me he would, but then he continued to do it."[279]

While only Joey and Peppermint slept with List, all four of the boys had to deal with List's orneriness. "I've looked for a redeeming quality in him, and I never could find one," Statton says. "He never showed any affection toward anyone. Nothing. It was just 'Here's what I want from you, and here's what I am willing to give you for it.' And ultimately I think that's what caused his demise."[280]

One night, after List had gone to bed, the four young men sat up late with a jug and some smokes. One of them joked that they "should just kill the old son of a bitch." They all laughed, but something about the remark must have taken.

The next morning, Statton cooked List the same hearty breakfast he always enjoyed, and all in the house would later say that List seemed to be in a good mood, at least by his standards.

List had no clue what he had left behind him that day.

Smiley and List had not gotten along from the start, and the street-tough Smiley bristled when List ordered him to scrub the terrazzo tiles. Smiley told the others that he wasn't scrubbing any floors. In fact, Smiley said, he was going to totally trash the whole place and split.

First went the china, hurled through the windows. Then Peppermint joined in on the fun, and the two hurled a huge potted plant from the second-floor veranda into the swimming pool. Chandeliers and a dining room wall bit the dust.[281]

And in that moment, Smiley decided he wouldn't be leaving until he had killed Bill List. He soon enlisted Jeff and Joey in his plan. Tim was in, too, though more halfheartedly. "I don't think we would have killed him if Smiley hadn't been there," Statton says. "That's not an excuse, but the original plan was just to trash the place and leave."[282]

That no longer sufficed for Smiley, who grabbed a pen and scrawled a statement of intent on a bedroom wall: "Bill List's a very sick man. He is going to die. Smiley 1984."[283]

"We all had our reasons, and we were all in it together, and that made it that much easier to plan it and for us to agree that it needed to be done," says Statton. "Now that I'm fifty years old, I look back and think, 'My God, what were we thinking?'"[284]

For the next four hours, the orgy of destruction raged, and after setting aside some toys they wanted to keep—a VCR and a stereo—they went to List's closet and grabbed his shotgun and a box of shells. Joey volunteered to be the triggerman, but the others told him he was too young. Statton and Peppermint demurred. Smiley leaped at the chance and posted up just inside the door as the evening shadows gathered.

At 5:45 p.m., as List got out of his Pontiac and was mounting the stairs to walk in the door, Smiley blew his head apart with a single shotgun blast. Minutes later, Statton saw Smiley pissing on List's corpse. After halfheartedly concealing the body, the four jumped in a car and drove off, the tape deck blaring Tina Turner. They had some cash, a couple of List's credit cards and, after using a stolen key to enter List's workplace, a company checkbook.[285]

Peppermint fled home to Illinois, courtesy of a plane ticket purchased with List's credit card. The other three went on a Montrose spree. Smiley decked himself out in a new suit and Joey a pair of leather pants. A heroin dealer cheated the trio out of $200, and then, when they tried to cash a check at an icehouse, an off-duty cop who worked there part time called List's company to verify it. The cop was told that List was dead, and the check was no good. There the spree ended.[286]

Smiley is currently serving a life sentence in the maximum-security Polunsky Unit, where he reportedly got married. Joey was sentenced to juvenile probation. Statton says Joey has been in and out of prison for most of his adult life, with his most recent stint ending in July 2012. Peppermint fought extradition from Illinois. When Texas authorities learned that he was dying of AIDS, extradition proceedings were dropped. He passed away in the 1990s.

Danny Lee Garrett died in prison in 1993, and Karla Faye Tucker was executed in 1998. If you are wondering how they are connected to this story, Deborah Thornton, the woman Tucker pickaxed to death while reportedly having a series of intense orgasms, was Bill List's estranged daughter.[287]

After standing vacant for several years, during which it was frequently used as a party house by area teens, and serving as the set for a B movie, the mansion was torn down. A gated community of Mediterranean-themed

McMansions stands on the site today, and in 2014, a man who leased one of the properties won the right to break that contract when he belatedly learned the history of the grounds on which his home stood. (A Facebook group called "Todville Murder Mansion" has more than two thousand members, the vast majority of them forty-somethings who recalled partying in the bizarre and sinister vacant pleasure palace by the bay.)[288]

As for Statton, for his role in the murder, he was convicted of nothing more than credit card abuse. Paroled three years into his fifteen-year sentence, Statton was in and out of jails for drug offenses in Texas and his native Kentucky until five years ago, when, he says, he cleaned up his act.[289]

Statton is remorseful but not exactly wracked by guilt. "No nightmares or anything like that," he says. Since his imprisonment, he's become a close personal friend of Elmer Wayne Henley, Dean Corll's serial-killing assistant and eventually Corll's killer. Statton believes that List was another Corll in the making.[290]

"It's not like I killed some grandma with four cats and a bunch of kids, and I just hated her and wanted her money. He was not the greatest person in the world," Statton says. "The district attorney told me, 'We're not trying to put you away for life. We're glad the motherfucker's dead,' and the Seabrook police chief said the same thing. But it was still a horrible thing to do."[291]

12
THE WIG SHOP MURDER

Jazz Age America was gripped by the epic trial of Leopold and Loeb, two well-heeled Jewish teens from Chicago who kidnapped and murdered a young friend just because they wanted to attempt the perfect crime. To save them from the death penalty, their families hired Clarence Darrow, then America's most famous and eloquent defense attorney. Darrow's impassioned speeches swayed the judge, and the thrill killers' lives were spared.

Seventy-four years later, Houston would suffer its own version of the Leopold and Loeb case. Dror Haim Goldberg, a troubled teen from a broken home in one of the city's toniest suburbs, barged into a West University Place wig shop and carved up three employees for reasons that remain known only to Goldberg himself. To mitigate his punishment, Goldberg's parents hired Dick DeGuerin, Houston's most famous and eloquent defense attorney, and in this case, as in several other high-profile murders, DeGuerin would be matched against the flamboyant Kelly Siegler, then a rising star of the prosecution bar and today the host of TNT's *Cold Justice* reality show.

Despite the horrific nature of Goldberg's crime and the fact that he embarked on a globe-spanning backpacking trek even as he knew the Houston Police Department was closing in on making his arrest, Goldberg was sentenced to neither death nor life in prison.

November 27, 1998—the day after Thanksgiving, Buy Nothing Day—was an unseasonably warm one even for subtropical Houston. At around four o'clock in the afternoon, it was almost eighty degrees, the sun baking the pavement at the Weslayan Plaza Shopping Center, just north of Houston's Mayberry-with-a-Visa-Black-card enclave city of West University Place. Wigs by Andre sits at the back of the complex, perpendicular to its anchor, a Randall's Flagship supermarket. Inside, employees Manuela Silverio, Roberta Ingrando and her husband, Roland, were winding down another long business day.[292]

Suddenly, the doors opened, and Silverio and Mrs. Ingrando saw a young man who had come in earlier and left without saying a word. He had nothing to say this time either. As Mrs. Ingrando would later testify, he strode directly to Ms. Silverio and "punched" her in the neck. Mrs. Ingrando ran to the phone and dialed 911. Goldberg slashed at her hand with what she now knew was a knife, causing her to drop the phone. Goldberg continued his attack, stabbing and cutting at Mrs. Ingrando. "Do you like it?" he asked her at one point. At another point, he said he would "make her pretty" by slashing her nose and ears. Hearing his wife's screams, Roland Ingrando came running from the office at the rear of the store, threw a tray of hair rollers at Goldberg and closed ranks to grapple with the teen; though he cut and slashed the unarmed Mr. Ingrando, Goldberg fled the store, ran across the parking lot and hopped into a dark Lincoln Navigator. A witness—Dr. Randall Beckman—tossed a bag of dog food purchased at a nearby pet store into his Volkswagen Golf, got in and followed the Navigator, taking note of its plates and eyeballing the driver in the process. Dr. Beckman then turned around and headed over to Wigs by Andre.[293]

There, he found the scene of a massacre. The bloodied Mr. and Mrs. Ingrando were frantically trying to call police. Silverio, age fifty-four, was already dead, splayed on the floor with 1.7 liters of her blood pooled inside her lifeless body. (Roland Ingrando's injuries were minor, but his wife, who was stabbed fourteen times, required life-saving emergency surgery and spent a week in the hospital.)[294]

"It was vicious," Houston police sergeant George Aldrete said near the time of the attack. "We don't know the exact reason for it, but we suspect (the killer) may have done it for the pure pleasure of killing somebody."[295]

Beckman gave police a description of the driver—white male, around six feet tall, slim, short, sandy-blonde hair, around eighteen years old. He also gave them the Navigator's license plate—1WL V84—which came back to a woman named Loren Nelson, the girlfriend of Goldberg's father, Dr. Isaac Goldberg, a prominent obstetrician-gynecologist. Between five

Wigs by Andre, looking rather unchanged since 1998. *From Gail Singer.*

and seven Columbia blue squad cars descended on Nelson's address: 2202 Dunstan Street, a 1938 brick bungalow in Southampton, then the favored neighborhood of Houston's go-go, but imminently doomed, Enron execs. Police found the Navigator parked behind the house, its engine still warm, the keys in the house. There was no sign of Goldberg. The housekeeper told police that Nelson and Dr. Goldberg were out of town and that young Dror was in charge of the place while they were away.

At 6:07 p.m., Goldberg drove up to the house in his own car—a white pickup truck. From about 4:30 p.m. to 5:45 p.m., immediately after the massacre, he'd been playing sandlot football with his buddies. Upon confirming his identity, officers cuffed Goldberg and read him his Miranda rights. Though not the murder weapon, police found a double-edged dagger under the seat of Goldberg's truck.

On the way to the police station, Goldberg told the cops a laughable story—that an unknown miscreant had stolen the Navigator on several prior occasions but had always returned the swanky SUV to its rightful owners once his or her errands were done. Faced with a photo array, Dr. Beckman said he was 80 percent certain Goldberg had been behind the wheel of the Navigator near the wig shop.

You can't say Goldberg's family—and even law enforcement—did not see this coming. Three years earlier, Dror Goldberg had predicted this very crime in writing. Houston Independent School District Police had seen it with their own eyes.

At 10:30 a.m. on April 10, 1995, HISD officer Duggan was patrolling the parking lot at Bellaire High School when he was almost hit by a beer can Goldberg tossed out his car window. (Unlike Leopold and Loeb, child prodigies with off-the-charts IQs and accomplishments to match, Goldberg was a mediocre student and athlete who excelled, if you can call it that, at partying. To be fair, a former manager at a West U–area Italian restaurant said that Goldberg was one of the best employees he ever had.) Duggan and fellow officer Griest apprehended the sixteen-year-old and found several more full beer cans in a cooler in the trunk and three joints in Goldberg's ashtray, along with a small knife on a keychain. Goldberg was taken to the assistant principal's office, where a conference with his parents awaited. Goldberg's backpack was seized and searched, and in looking for LSD or smashed marijuana buds, Officer Griest examined several spiral notebooks. What she found inside chilled her to the bone.

As she would later testify, there was a drawing of the devil with blood "all over it and blood everywhere, and it was just—it was striking." She turned the page and found an essay of sorts entitled "How to Kill a Woman."

"It...talked about abducting," she testified in response to questions from prosecutor Kelly Siegler. "It wasn't a poem, it wasn't a letter, and it took you from beginning to end. Talked about using a knife to make several cuts so that when she bled, the body would be covered, I mean, in red. Talked about her begging for her life. You could feel it. I mean, it was disturbing. Talked about her begging for her life and then the joy when she looked into his eyes and he realized they were dead and that he had no use for the bitch."

Siegler then asked if she remembers any of the words that Goldberg fantasized about himself using.

"Yes," Griest replied. "Goldberg planned to say things like, 'Do you like it? Want me to do it some more? I'm going to do this.' Just really talking. It was very talkative to the victim while she was being stabbed. Very tormenting. [The notebook described] how she would sweat, how her eyes would look, just the terror. You could—it was like reading the best novel you've ever read in your life."

Elsewhere in the same notebook, Goldberg penned another work entitled "How to Rape a Woman." "Talking about during penetration putting hands around her neck and her begging him stop, her begging him till she couldn't beg anymore because her airflow was getting cut off and getting erect when he let go right before her body—right before, I guess, he said lifeless and she would gasp for air and sexually turn him on," Griest recalled. She said that Goldberg wrote that these urges were overwhelming him and that he was contemplating suicide.

"How can you write such sick shit?" Griest asked at the time.

"I have thoughts," Goldberg replied.

The notebooks were handed over to Goldberg's parents. Thanks to the little keychain knife, Goldberg was placed on juvenile probation.

At his trial, other letters would come forth, no less disturbing. In a letter to an Israeli friend, Goldberg seethes with rage over bomb attacks in Tel Aviv and yearns for vengeance. "The fact that I may be given a chance to kill an enemy of our state is keeping me going. [Loren Nelson] has noticed the change in my behavior and rarely stops to talk to me. She says I scare her. No offense, Josh, but sometimes I want to pop her head like a zit." After some small talk, Goldberg abruptly changes tack: "I am now dating a slut named Christina. I want to cut her throat. I am changing into a violent young man, and I like it. I pray you do well, and pray you keep your health. Remember, Josh, you wanted this very badly. How dare a bunch of sand niggers hurt us. Kill them all."

Police released Goldberg just before midnight on November 27, the night of the slaying. According to a court document, his mother smacked him for talking to police.

Goldberg, a dual United States–Israeli citizen, flew to Israel in December and returned to America in January 1998. By the time he was indicted in February 1998, he was gone again, to Thailand this time. Goldberg traveled the world for the next five months, his arrest finally coming in the Frankfurt airport just as he was about to board a Mexico City–bound plane. (Goldberg's parents later stated they had not known his whereabouts during that five-month period.) Three months later, Goldberg was flown back to Houston alongside several United States marshals.[296]

Goldberg's trial got underway in the spring of 2000. The evidence against him was fairly overwhelming. Siegler and co-prosecutor Lester Buzzard had four eyewitnesses putting Goldberg at or near the crime scene. Lab techs found wig fibers matching some from the shop inside the Navigator, which was festooned with a license plate handed over to police by an eyewitness. Police testified about the warmth of the SUV's engine when they arrived at Dunstan. Goldberg had no credible alibi for his whereabouts between 3:50 p.m. and 4:30 p.m. Siegler also presented his deeply disturbed writings and questionable post-murder globe-trotting in making her case.

DeGuerin, less a flamboyant orator than tenacious bulldog of a defense attorney, attempted to discredit every bit of damning evidence against his client. As an attorney pal of his once put it, DeGuerin's ethic is to "proclaim the innocence of the client to the last syllable of recorded time." He attempted to discredit the police lineups as being biased against Goldberg and claimed that Mrs. Ingrando's identification of Goldberg was tentative and the result of being asked leading questions. DeGuerin said that eighteen dark-colored Navigators with very similar license plates had been sold at a nearby dealership and pointed out that there was no blood or DNA evidence linking Goldberg to the crime. The letter to the Israeli friend? Goldberg was enraged over the Palestinian bombings. Plus, who could ever believe that a handsome doctor's son from one of Houston's wealthiest neighborhoods would butcher one woman and attempt to slaughter another woman in cold blood? (Goldberg's team would later claim in an appeal that "How to Kill a Woman" and "How to Rape a Woman" had been obtained through an illegal search. The appeal was denied.)

On April 14, 2000, after seventeen hours of deliberation, the jury returned with a guilty verdict. While Goldberg showed little emotion, his relatives and those of Silverio wept. One of Goldberg's buddies tried to cold-cock a news photographer as the families gathered in a hallway outside the courtroom. DeGuerin said he was "very, very disappointed." Siegler and Buzzard cited a gag order and declined comment, but in her closing argument, Siegler left us with the questions an entire city has been trying to answer since Buy Nothing Day 1998, the same questions Chicago and the nation grappled with in Leopold and Loeb's wake in 1924.

"Their defense is you have to have a reasonable doubt because how can you believe that someone like Dror Goldberg who's so nice looking, who's so educated, who's so intelligent, with the wonderful, beautiful mother and prestigious doctor dad and the loving stepmother and two loving brothers raised in Bellaire, Texas, with all that money and that position and everything the world had to offer, how could you believe that someone who looks like him could do a murder like this?"[297]

Since the case was not filed as capital murder, Goldberg was faced with anything from probation to life behind bars. He wound up with forty-eight years, a sentence confirmed on appeal, and is currently serving time in the Stringfellow Unit, a former prison farm not far from Sugar Land.[298]

NOTES

CHAPTER 1

1. Stephen L. Hardin, *Texian Macabre* (Buffalo Gap, TX: State House Press, 2007).
2. John Hunter Herndon Diary, 1838, Eugene C. Barker Papers, University of Texas at Austin. Diary also appeared in *Southwest Historical Quarterly* 53 no. 3 (January 1950), edited by Andrew Forest Muir; Hardin, *Texian Macabre*.
3. Stephen Hardin interview with the authors, October 6, 2012.
4. Max Freund, ed., *Gustav Dresel's Houston Journal* (Austin: University of Texas Press, 1954); John Hoyt Williams, *Sam Houston: A Biography of the Father of Texas* (New York: Simon and Schuster, 1993).
5. Freund, *Dresel Journal*.
6. Herndon diary.
7. Hardin interview.
8. Ibid.; Herndon diary.
9. Hardin interview.
10. Ibid.
11. Leslie H. Southwick, "Grayson, Peter," Handbook of Texas Online, http://www.tshaonline.org/handbook/online/articles/fgr29 (accessed February 11, 2014); Herbert Gambrell, *Anson Jones: The Last President of Texas* (Austin: University of Texas Press, 1947).
12. Joe E. Erichson, "Collingsworth, George Morse," Handbook of Texas Online, http://www.tshaonline.org/handbook/online/articles/fco97.

13. Louis Wiltz Kemp, *The Signers of the Texas Declaration of Independence* (Houston: Anson Jones Press, 1944); Joe E. Erichson, "Childress, George Campbell," Handbook of Texas Online, http://www.tshaonline.org/handbook/online/articles/fch28 (accessed February 11, 2014).

14. Kemp, *Signers*; Priscilla Meyers Benham, "Rusk, Thomas," Handbook of Texas Online, http://www.tshaonline.org/handbook/online/articles/fru16 (accessed February 11, 2014).

15. Herbert Gambrell, "Jones, Anson," Handbook of Texas Online, http://www.tshaonline.org/handbook/online/articles/fjo42 (accessed February 11, 2014); Gambrell, *Anson Jones*.

16. Audrey Barrett Cook, *Obedience Smith: Pioneer of Three American Frontiers* (Houston: Early Publishing Company, 2008); Herndon diary; Hardin interview.

17. *Telegraph and Texas Register*, August 19, 1837.

18. Madge Thornall Roberts, ed., *The Personal Correspondence of Sam Houston* (Denton: University of North Texas Press, 1996).

19. Malcolm D. McLean, *Fine Texas Horses: Their Pedigrees and Performance, 1830–1845* (Fort Worth: Texas Christian University Monographs, 1966).

20. *Telegraph and Texas Register*, October 20, 1838; Thomas W. Cutrer, "Wharton, John Austin," Handbook of Texas Online, http://www.tshaonline.org/handbook/online/articles/fba77 (accessed February 11, 2014).

21. Hardin, *Texian Macabre*; *Telegraph and Texas Register*, July 17, 1839; *Telegraph and Texas Register*, October 2, 1839

22. Ashbel Smith papers, December 20, 1838, Dolph Briscoe Center for American History, University of Texas–Austin.

23. McLean, *Fine Texas Horses*.

24. *Brazos Courier*, April 21, 1840; *Austin City Gazette*, May 6, 1840.

25. Freund, *Dresel Journal*.

26. Cook, *Obedience Smith*; Freund, *Dresel Journal*.

CHAPTER 2

27. *Houston Tri-Weekly Telegraph*, July 21, 1862.

28. Arthur Freemantle, *Three Months in the Southern States, April–June 1863* (Mobile, AL: S.H. Goetzel, 1864).

29. Paul D. Casdorph, *Prince John Magruder* (New York: John Wiley & Sons, 1996); John B. Magruder to Edmund Kirby Smith, Beaumont,

September 26, 1863; *War of the Rebellion: A Compilation of the Official Records of the Union and Confederate Armies*, series 1, vol. 26, pt. 2 (Washington, D.C.: Government Printing Office, 1880–1901), 261.

30. Ralph A. Wooster, "Civil War," Handbook of Texas Online, https://www.tshaonline.org/handbook/online/articles/qdc02 (accessed January 28, 2014).

31. Robert P. Perkins, *John Robert Baylor: The Life and Times of Arizona's Confederate Governor* (Phoenix, AZ: Colonel Sherod Hunter Camp, Sons of Confederate Veterans, 1999–2007).

32. United States Census, 1860, Parker County, Texas; Wooster, "Civil War."

33. William Wharton Groce, "Major General John A. Wharton," *Southwestern Historical Quarterly* 19 (January 1916).

34. Robert Maberry Jr., "Barr, Robert," Handbook of Texas Online, http://www.tshaonline.org/handbook/online/articles/fwh04 (accessed January 29, 2014).

35. *Galveston Daily News*, March 19, 1865; *Galveston Weekly News*, April 5, 1865.

36. Ron Soodalter, "Murder in the Civil War," *America's Civil War Magazine* (July 2010); William Pitt Ballinger Diary, April 9, 1865; Cook, *Obedience Smith*.

37. *Flake's Daily Bulletin*, May 21, 1868; Groce, "John A. Wharton."

38. *Flake's Daily Bulletin*, May 22, 1868; Houston City Directory, 1866, comp. W.A. Leonard (Houston: Gray, Strickland & Co., Printers); Isabella Margaret Blandin, *History of Shearn Church, 1837–1907* (n.p.: Shearn's Auxiliary of Women's Home Mission Society, 1907).

39. *Houston Tri-Weekly Telegraph*, April 10, 1865.

40. *Flake's Daily Bulletin*, May 21 and 22, 1868.

41. John B. Magruder quoted in *Houston Telegraph* without a date in William W. White, "The Disintegration of an Army: Confederate Forces in Texas, April–June 1865," *East Texas Historical Journal* 26 (Fall 1988).

42. H.A. Wallace, "Reminiscences of the Last Vestige of a Lost Cause," 1865, Dolph Briscoe Center for American History, University of Texas–Austin.

43. Charles William Ramsdell, *Reconstruction in Texas* (Austin: Texas State Historical Association, 1910).

44. *Houston Telegraph*, May 19, 1868.

45. *Flake's Daily Bulletin*, May 21 and 22, 1868.

46. *Houston Telegraph*, December 6, 1868.

47. Walter Prescott Webb, *The Texas Rangers* (Boston: Houghton Mifflin, 1935); Wooster, "Civil War"; Robert Utley, *Lone Star Justice* (New York: Berkley Books, 2002).

48. Freedmen's Bureau Records, "Miscellaneous Records Relating to Murders and Other Criminal Offenses Committed in Texas 1865–1868," National Archives Microfilm Publication, M821 Roll 32.

49. Dr. Samuel O. Young, *True Stories of Old Houston and Houstonians* (Galveston, TX: Oscar Springer, 1913).

50. Barry Crouch, "All the Vile Passions: The Texas Black Code of 1866," *Southwestern Historical Quarterly* 97 (July 1993); *Houston Tri-Weekly Telegraph*, November 29, 1865.

51. *Flake's Daily Bulletin*, May 22, 1868.

52. Freedmen's Bureau, M821 Roll 32; United States Census, 1860, Montgomery County, Texas.

53. Freedmen's Bureau, M821 Roll 32; United States Census, 1860, Montgomery County, Texas.

54. *Official Records*, series 1, vol. 48, pt. 1, 301; Ramsdell, *Reconstruction in Texas*.

55. Freedmen's Bureau, M821 Roll 32.

56. *Evening Star* (Houston, TX), April 30, 1866.

57. General William E. Strong to General Oliver O. Howard, January 1, 1866. House Executive Documents, 39th Congress, 1st Session, Document 70.

58. Freedmen's Bureau, M821 Roll 32; United States Census, 1860, Brazoria County, Texas.

59. Young, *True Stories*; Ramsdell, *Reconstruction in Texas*.

Chapter 3

60. *Yale Alumni Magazine* (1873); William Pitt Riddell Papers, Manuscript 604, Louisiana Research Collection, Tulane University; United States Census, 1870, Harris County, Texas; *Galveston Daily News*, May 24, 1872.

61. *Galveston Daily News*, May 24, 1872.

62. Ibid.

63. *Houston Telegraph*, May 30, 1872.

64. Ibid.

65. *Galveston Daily News*, November 19, 1875.

66. *New York Times*, February 9, 1886.

67. *Houston Post*, February 9, 1886.

68. Ibid.

69. Ibid.

70. *Houston Post*, February 11, 1886.

71. Nelson Zoch, *Badge and Gun*, Houston Police Officers' Union magazine (September 2007).

72. Pauline Yelderman, *The Jay Bird Democratic Association of Fort Bend County: A White Man's Union* (Waco: Texian Press, 1979).

73. Ibid.

74. Ibid.

75. Clarence Wharton, *History of Fort Bend County* (San Antonio, TX: Naylor, 1939).

76. Yelderman, *Jay Bird*; Wharton, *History of Fort Bend*.

77. *Houston Post*, April 30, 1897

78. *Houston Post*, May 1, 1897.

79. Ibid.

80. Ibid; *Houston Post*, May 2, 1897.

81. *Houston Post*, May 1, 1897.

82. Ibid.

83. *Houston Post*, May 2, 1897; *Sacramento Record Union*, May 1, 1897; *Norfolk Virginian*, May 1, 1897.

84. *Houston Post*, May 3, 1897.

85. *Galveston Daily News*, May 3, 1897; *Houston Post*, May 4 1897.

86. *Houston Post*, May 15, 1897.

87. Handbook of Texas Online, "Eldridge, William," http://www.tshaonline.org/handbook/online/articles/fel33 (accessed February 12, 2014).

88. Diana J. Kleiner, "Imperial Sugar Company," Handbook of Texas Online, http://www.tshaonline.org/handbook/online/articles/diicy (accessed February 12, 2014).

Chapter 4

89. *Houston Chronicle*, March 18, 1910.

90. *Houston Post*, March 16, 1910.

91. Harris County Coroner's Inquest Book, JP1, March 16, 1910, 73; *Houston Post*, March 16, 1910; *Houston Post*, March 17, 1910.

92. Key to the City of Houston, City Federation of Women's Clubs, 209 (1908).

93. *Houston Post*, March 17, 1910; *Abilene Semi-Weekly Reporter*, June 16, 1911.

94. *Houston Post*, March 17, 1910; Coroner's Inquest Book. Note: Schultz's nickname also appears as "Tad."

95. *Houston Post*, March 17, 1910.

96. Ibid.; *Houston Post*, March 18, 1910.

97. Ibid.; Ibid.

98. Ibid.; Ibid.

99. *Houston Courier*, March 19, 1910; *Houston Post*, March 22, 1910.

100. *Houston Post*, March 18, 1910; *Houston Courier*, March 18, 1910.

101. *Houston Post*, March 19, 1910; *Houston Post*, March 22, 1910; *Houston Post*, March 23, 1910.

102. National Institute of Justice, *Fingerprint Sourcebook*, July 2011; *Houston Post*, March 19, 1910.

103. *Houston Post*, March 24, 1910; *Houston Post*, March 26, 1910; Houston City Directory, 1910. Note: Frank Turney was first identified as Turner.

104. *Abilene Reporter*, June 16, 1911; *Houston Post*, June 13, 1911.

105. *Houston Post*, June 14, 1911.

106. *Houston Post*, June 13, 1911; *Houston Post*, June 14, 1911.

107. *Houston Post*, June 14, 1911.

108. *Galveston Daily News*, October 3, 1911.

109. *Houston Post*, December 5, 1911; *Houston Post*, April 2, 1912; Harris County Criminal Courts Case #17596, July 5, 1911.

110. Harris County Court Cases #17599–603 of 1911, filing of October 11, 1912.

111. *Galveston Daily News*, May 14, 1913.

112. United States Census, 1910, 1920, 1930, Harris County, Texas; Texas Death Certificate.

113. United States Census, 1910, Harris County, Texas, 167; Houston City Directories, 1913–17; Texas Department of State Health Services, "About San Antonio State Hospital," http://www.dshs.state.tx.us/mhhospitals/SanAntonioSH/SASH_About.shtm (accessed April 14, 2014).

114. HCCC #17599–603.

115. United States Census, 1920, 1930, 1940, Harris County, Texas; *San Antonio Express*, March 30, 1941; Texas Death Certificate.

CHAPTER 5

116. United States Census, 1920, Harris County, Texas, Roll 1813:128; *Houston Post*, April 21, 1922; Courthouse records, Texas Marriages 1837–1973, vol. 17, 110.

117. Harris County Inquest Books, JP Pct 1, April 19, 1922; *Houston Post*, April 21, 1922.

118. *Houston Post*, April 22, 1922; *Houston Post*, September 20, 1922.

119. San Marcos Academy catalogue (1921).

120. *Houston Post*, September 21, 1922.

121. Harris County District Court Cases 25406, 25418, filed 1922; *San Antonio Express*, September 19, 1922.

122. *Houston Post*, September 20, 1922.

123. Ibid.

124. *San Antonio Express*, September 19, 1922.

125. *Houston Post*, September 20, 1922; *Houston Post*, September 21, 1922.

126. *Galveston Daily News*, September 20, 1922.

127. Ibid.

128. *Houston Post*, September 21, 1922.

129. HCDCC #25406; *Houston Post*, September 21, 1922.

130. *Houston Post*, September 22, 1922.

131. *San Antonio Express*, September 22, 1922.

132. Harris County Inquest Book, JP1 Glenn Fuller, April 2, 1931.

133. HC Inquests, Strebeck, Hosey, Hart and Williams cases, 1931.

134. HC Inquests, Dismuke, June 10, 1931.

135. HC Inquests, March 17, 1931.

136. HC Inquests, April 13, 1931.

CHAPTER 6

137. Ann Becker, *Houston: 1860–1900* (Charleston, SC: Arcadia Publishing, 2010).

138. H.M. Hobbs Scrapbook, Harris County Archives; Paul Schneider, *Bonnie and Clyde: The Lives Behind the Legend* (New York: St. Martin's Griffin, 2010); *Houston Press*, May 1933; *Houston Press*, March 26, 1930.

139. Schneider, *Bonnie and Clyde*; *Houston Post*, March 29, 1930; United States Census, 1930, McClennan County, Texas; United States Census, 1930, Harris County, Texas.

140. *Houston Press*, May 1933.

141. *Houston Post*, July 3, 1929.

142. *Houston Post*, March 26, 1930.

143. HCCCC #33660, filed April 16, 1930.

144. HCCCC #33660; HCCCC #33661.

145. *Houston Post*, March 29, 1930; *Houston Post*, April 1, 1930; *Houston Post*, April 3, 1930; *Houston Post*, April 4, 1930.

146. *Houston Press*, August 21, 1930; *Wichita Daily Times*, August 21, 1930; HCCCC #33660.

147. Harris County Juvenile Court Docket; United States Census, 1910, Ellis County, Texas.

148. Houston City Directory, 1918; United States Census Harris County, 1920, Texas; *Lubbock Avalanche Journal*, May 24, 1934.

149. United States Census, 1910, Midland, Nolan and Tom Green Counties, Texas; United States Census, 1920, Harris County, Texas.

150. Hobbs scrapbook.

151. Hobbs scrapbook; *Houston Press*, December 4, 1933.

152. Hobbs scrapbook.

153. *Houston Press*, January 19, 1934.

154. Hobbs scrapbook; *Houston Post*, January 19, 1934.

155. Phillip W. Steele and Marie Barrow Scoma, *The Family Story of Bonnie and Clyde* (New Orleans: Pelican Publishing, 2000); author interviews with Robert Schaadt, Gene Wiggins, Robert Scherer and Kevin Ladd, June and July 2014.

156. Letter from Wharton County Sheriff to Dallas, Texas Bureau of Identification, Dallas County Archives.

157. Jeff Guinn, *Go Down Together* (New York: Simon & Schuster, 2009); Bartee Haile, *Texas Depression-Era Desperadoes* (Charleston, SC: The History Press, 2014); Texas Hideout, http://texashideout.tripod.com/ray.html (accessed June 25, 2014).

158. Hobbs scrapbook.

159. Guinn, *Go Down Together*; Hobbs scrapbook.

160. Guinn, *Go Down Together*.

161. Hobbs scrapbook; *Houston Post*, April 2, 1934; *Mexia Daily News*, September 19, 1950.

162. *Houston Post*, April 2, 1934; Hobbs scrapbook.

163. Hobbs scrapbook.

164. Guinn, *Go Down Together*; Hobbs scrapbook.

165. *Spartanburg (SC) Journal*, April 6, 1935; John Neal Phillips, *Running with Bonnie and Clyde* (Norman: University of Oklahoma Press, 1996).

166. Phillips, *Running with Bonnie and Clyde*; Hobbs scrapbook.

167. Phillips, *Running with Bonnie and Clyde*; Mary Carey, "The Impossible Interview," *Argosy*, February 1958.

168. Guinn, *Go Down Together*; *Houston Post*, April 4, 1934.

169. *Houston Post*, April 5, 1934; Phillips, *Running with Bonnie and Clyde*; Guinn, *Go Down Together*.

170. Guinn, *Go Down Together*; Phillips, *Running with Bonnie and Clyde*; Schneider, *Bonnie and Clyde*.

171. Guinn, *Go Down Together*; Phillips, *Running with Bonnie and Clyde*; *Houston Press*, April 4, 1934.

172. Hobbs scrapbook; *Houston Post*, February 21, 1935; *Reading (PA) Eagle*, February 23, 1935.

173. *State Times Advocate* (Baton Rouge), February 2, 1933; *Houston Post*, February 3, 1933; *New Orleans Times-Picayune*, March 14, 1933.

174. *Texas Department of Criminal Justice* (Nashville: Turner Publishing, 2004); Hobbs scrapbook; *Houston Post*, February 3, 1933.

175. Phillips, *Running with Bonnie and Clyde*; Carey, *Impossible Interview*.

176. Ibid.; Ibid.

177. Carey, "Impossible Interview."

178. Hobbs scrapook; *Miami News*, March 31, 1935; Phillips, *Running with Bonnie and Clyde*.

179. Hobbs scrapbook.

180. *Houston Press*, April 4, 1935.

181. Carey, "Impossible Interview"; Phillips, *Running with Bonnie and Clyde*.

182. Phillips, *Running with Bonnie and Clyde*; Hobbs scrapbook.

183. W.D. Jones, "Bonnie and Clyde," *Playboy* (November 1968); Guinn, *Go Down Together*.

184. Jones, "Bonnie and Clyde."

185. *Lubbock Avalanche*, November 26, 1933; Jones, "Bonnie and Clyde."

186. Jones, "Bonnie and Clyde."

187. William Daniel Jones, Texas Death Certificate; *Houston Courier*, October 4, 1974.

CHAPTER 7

188. Robert Bentley, *Dangerous Games* (New York: Birch Lane Press, 1993).

189. Ibid.

190. James T. Sears, *Rebels, Rubyfruit, and Rhinestones: Queering Space in the Stonewall South* (Piscataway, NJ: Rutgers University Press, 2001).

191. Bentley, *Dangerous Games*.

192. Ibid.

193. Ibid.

194. Marilyn Underwood, "Rodriguez, Josefa (Chipita)," Handbook of Texas Online, http://www.tshaonline.org/handbook/online/articles/fro50 (accessed March 24, 2014).

195. *El Paso Herald Post*, February 2, 1966.

196. Internet Movie Database, "The Carolyn Lima Story," http://www.imdb.com/title/tt0212044 (accessed July 5, 2014); *El Paso Herald Post*, November 5, 1965.

197. *El Paso Herald Post*, February 2, 1966.

198. *Houston Chronicle*, March 14, 1991; Texas Political Almanac, http://www.txpoliticalalmanac.com/index.php?title=Annise_Parker (accessed July 9, 2014); Bentley, *Dangerous Games*.

Chapter 8

199. Author interview with Dr. Denton and Louise Cooley, January 12, 2013; author interview with Susan Cooley, January 16, 2013; author interview with Carolyn "Honey Bear" Wolters, January 10, 2013.

200. Craig Malisow, "Jonestown's Medicine Man," *Houston Press*, January 30, 2013.

201. *Houston Post*, September 16, 1959.

202. Susan Cooley interview.

203. *Houston Post*, September 16, 1959.

204. Ibid.

205. Ibid.

206. Author interview with Sherrie Tatum, September 22, 2012.

207. Author interview with Bill Thomas, January 17, 2013.

208. Ibid.

209. Ibid.

210. Susan Cooley interview; Wolters interview.

211. Malisow, "Jonestown's Medicine Man."

212. Jim Garrison, *On the Trail of the Assassins* (New York: Sheridan Square Press, 1988).

213. Warren Commission Report 1964; Anthony Summers, *Not in Your Lifetime* (n.p.: Marlowe & Co., 1998).

214. John Craig and A. Phillip Rogers, *The Man on the Grassy Knoll* (New York: Avon, 1992).

215. Craig and Rogers, *Man on the Grassy Knoll*.

216. Ibid.

217. Tatum interview.

218. Ibid.

219. Ibid.

220. Ibid.

221. Malisow, "Jonestown's Medicine Man."

222. Tatum interview.

223. Ibid.

224. Larry Schacht affidavit in support of Jim Jones, August 1977.

225. Malisow, "Jonestown's Medicine Man."

226. Schacht affidavit.

227. FBI Memo, December 1978; Malisow, "Jonestown's Medicine Man."

228. FBI Memo, December 1978.

229. Schacht affidavit; Malisow, "Jonestown's Medicine Man."

230. Malisow, "Jonestown's Medicine Man."

231. Ibid.

232. Ibid.

233. Ibid.

Chapter 9

234. Thorn Dreyer, "Long Strange Trip: Austin's 13th Floor Elevators and Still Trippin' Tommy Hall," Rag Blog, 2009.

235. Jennifer Maerz, "A Long, Strange Trip," *San Francisco Weekly*, February 18, 2009; Dreyer, "Long Strange Trip."

236. Dreyer, "Long Strange Trip."

237. Ibid.

238. Ivan Koop Kuper, "Stacy and Bunni: A Montrose Love Story," Rag Blog, March 31, 2011; Maerz, "Long, Strange Trip."

239. Kuper, "Stacy and Bunni."

240. Ibid.; Maerz, "Long, Strange Trip."

241. Kuper, "Stacy and Bunni."

242. Ibid.

243. *Houston Chronicle*, August 25, 1978.

244. Ibid.

245. Kuper, "Stacy and Bunni."

246. *Kerrville Mountain Sun*, August 31, 1978.

Chapter 10

247. *Abilene Reporter News*, August 16, 1973; *Victoria Advocate*, August 19, 1973.

248. *Abilene Reporter News*, August 16, 1973.

249. Ibid.

250. Author interview with Victor Driscoll, October 18, 2013.

251. Ibid.

252. Ibid.

253. *Corsicana Daily Sun*, November 13, 1974.

254. *Mexia Daily News*, November 13, 1974; Driscoll interview.

255. *Big Spring Herald*, June 4, 1975.

256. *Houston Chronicle*, October 29, 2004.

257. Driscoll interview.

258. *Houston Chronicle*, October 29, 2004.

259. Driscoll interview; *Houston Chronicle*, May 23, 1975.

260. *Houston Chronicle*, May 23, 1975.

261. *Midland Reporter Telegram*, June 4, 1975; *Pampa Daily News*, November 3, 1974; Driscoll interview.

262. Driscoll interview.

263. Ibid.

264. *Big Spring Herald*, June 4, 1975.

265. *Houston Post*, June 4, 1975.

266. *Houston Chronicle*, June 5, 1975.

267. Driscoll interview.

268. *Corpus Christi Times*, July 16, 1974.

269. *Houston Chronicle*, April 1, 1984.

270. Driscoll interview.

Chapter 11

271. Author interview with Jeff Statton, October 8, 2012.

272. *Houston Chronicle*, "The Street that Led to Murder," November 18, 1985.

273. Angela Leicht, "The Five Most Sinister Mansions in the Houston Area," *Houston Press*, May 1, 2014.

274. Statton interview.

275. Ibid.

276. Ibid.

277. Ibid.; *Houston Chronicle*, "Street."

278. Statton interview.

279. Ibid.

280. Ibid.

281. *Houston Chronicle*, "Street."

282. Statton interview.

283. *Houston Chronicle*, "Street."

284. Statton interview.

285. *Houston Chronicle*, "Street."

286. Statton interview; *Houston Chronicle*, "Street."

287. Joseph Geringer, "Karla Faye Tucker: Texas' Controversial Murderess," Crime Library; Executed Today, "Karla Faye Tucker," http://www.executedtoday.com/2008/02/03/1998-karla-faye-tucker (accessed July 9, 2014).

288. Swamplot, "Man Who Almost Leased Home Built on Site of Todville Murder Mansion Wants His Money Back," http://swamplot.com/man-who-almost-leased-home-built-on-site-of-todville-murder-mansion-wants-his-money-back/2014-04-23 (accessed June 5, 2014); Travelers Today, "Bill List Todville Mansion," http://www.travelerstoday.com/articles/9626/20140425/bill-list-todville-mansion-photos-decades-old-murder-seabrook-texas.htm (accessed 5 June 5, 2014); Internet Movie Database, "The House on Todville Road," http://www.imdb.com/title/tt0110065 (accessed July 9, 2014).

289. Statton interview.

290. Ibid.

291. Ibid.

CHAPTER 12

292. *Amarillo Globe News*, April 16, 2000.

293. Texas Court of Appeals, Houston, Case #01-00-00628-CR, August 22, 2002.

294. Ibid.

295. *Kerrville Times*, December 19, 1999.

296. Texas Court of Appeals, Case # 01-00-00628-CR; *Amarillo Globe News*, April 16, 2000; *Daily Cougar*, University of Houston, April 15, 1999.

297. Amy Klein, "Houston Asks: 'Thrill Killer' or 'All-American'?" *Forward*, March 2, 2001.

298. Texas Court of Appeals, Case # 01-00-00628-CR; *Texas Tribune*, "Dror Haim Goldberg," http://www.texastribune.org/library/data/texas-prisons/inmates/dror-haim-goldberg/387060 (accessed April 16, 2014).

ABOUT THE AUTHORS

John Nova Lomax

John Nova Lomax is an associate editor at *Houstonia Magazine*, Houston's only city magazine. Previously, he was the music editor and later a staff writer at the *Houston Press*, where he frequently covered both high crimes and amusing misdemeanors for the paper and the "Hair Balls" blog. In 2008, he was awarded the ASCAP Deems Taylor Award for excellence in music journalism for his coverage of troubled former country music star Doug Supernaw. He really wishes Earl Campbell, Nolan Ryan and Hakeem Olajuwon were still playing ball and that Felix Mexican Restaurant was still dishing out Special Dinners.

MIKE VANCE

Mike Vance, a native Houstonian, is the executive director and founder of Houston Arts and Media, a non-profit organization that creates innovative ways to educate Texans about their history. Following a long career as a professional in radio, television, comedy, script writing, acting and music, Mike switched to another passion: chronicling history. To date, he is responsible for five books, four feature-length documentaries, over fifty history television shows, forty-one short videos on Houston history and a variety of bar tabs at local icehouses. Mike currently serves on the Harris County Historical Commission.